THE CATHEDRAL OF MEMORY

Volume I

Tracey Patrick Valmont

Grolee House
Opelousas, Louisiana

Published by Grolee House

Opelousas, Louisiana

First Edition, 2026

ISBN 979-8-234-04041-1

CATHEDRAL OF MEMORY

Dedication

To my sister, Beverly Christy —

This is yours before it belongs to anyone else. What you hold is not simply pages bound together, but the keeping of a promise: that our history would not be lost, that our stories would not go untold.

It began as so much does with families - a conversation, but in this instance we spoke about the Tuskegee Airmen — their place in the firmament of history, and the bitter irony that those once doubted are now quietly erased, their portraits removed from walls, their stories stricken from academic syllabi, and their names deleted from the very websites where they once stood as guardians of their own memory. And yet — where others erase, we remember. Where silence presses in, we speak.

Beverly, you know my love for writing: not performance, but preservation, as our grandparents once did at the table passing down recipes, traditions and truths about who we are so that black children would remember what the world preferred that everyone forget.

When I said to you "I will write something - but only if you want me to", you gave me permission to begin. What I called a short essay for you became a door to countless remembrances. One story opened into another, and then another, until I found myself standing inside a metaphorical cathedral built of memories.

This book and its essays form the first stone of that cathedral. You, Beverly, gave me the courage to lay it down.

And to the late Toni Morrison — who told us: "If there's a book that you want to read, but it hasn't been written yet, then you must write it." This work stands in her shadow, and in her light.

With love, always,
Tracey

Preface

Artistry is not confined to canvas or stage, nor to pen, nor to instrument. Artistry is who we are — the rhythm in our footsteps, the cadence in our speech, the beauty we carve from hardship, the dignity we carry even when the world would strip us bare.

We are the originators of this earth, bearers of the Eve gene, present at the beginning and enduring through every age. From our hands came the first tools; from our tongues came the first stories; from our songs came the first music. What the world calls "art" we have always called "life".

This Cathedral is no mere archive. It is a sanctuary built of remembrance — each chapter a pillar, each story a window of light, each name a stone in a structure that has been rising for two hundred years and more.

We live in a society so determined to restrain us that it unwittingly provided the stage upon which we displayed our brilliance. Those who doubted us became our witnesses and those who barred us from honor became the unwilling heralds of our greatness.

Let it be understood: artistry is not a profession. It is our inheritance. It is the marrow of our pride. And it is the unbroken thread that ties Phillis Wheatley to Maya Angelou, Benjamin Banneker to Katherine Johnson, Marian Anderson to Beyoncé and every unnamed ancestor to every child not yet born.

So let the world try to forget: we will remember. Let others diminish: we shall enlarge. And in doing so, just like the airmen of Tuskegee, we too shall soar.

What you hold is one volume of a larger work — the first stone of this Cathedral, the chapters that lay the foundation of Black achievement across art, science, education, and the human spirit.

The building continues.

The Cathedral of Memory
— A Poem —

We were here when the first dawn cracked the silence,
when rivers carved their names into stone,
when the drumbeat was not music but heartbeat,
and heartbeat was the measure of the world.

We were here before parchment,
before ink thought itself immortal,
before history claimed the arrogance of beginning.
We are beginning. We are origin. We are root.

Call this place a cathedral if you must —
but know its arches are our spines,
its pillars our stories,
its stained glass the shatter of chains refracted into
light.

Every window sings: Phillis, Douglass, Zora,
Baldwin, Morrison.
Every aisle hums with Carver's hands, Katherine
Johnson's numbers,
Bethune's classrooms, King's dream unfurled.
Their voices are not relics. They are choir.

And if you listen closely
You will hear the Red Tails roar above,
Engines stitched with defiance,
Guardian angels escorting every fragile hope home.

You will hear the pens scrape across centuries,
Writing us back into the books that forgot us,
You will hear laughter in kitchens,
Hymns in pews,
A mother's sharp "don't you quit" whispered like
gospel.

The Cathedral of Memory is not built of stone.
It is built of us —
Black hands that tilled,
Black minds that solved,
Black tongues that preached,
Black souls that refused silence.

So let the government strip our portraits from its walls,
Let it ban our names from academic syllabi,
Let it burn the books and choke on the smoke
But still we rise, still we write, still we sing.

Volume I

The great chapters of Black achievement,
artistry, and endurance

CHAPTER ONE

The Sky Was Never the Limit

A Tribute to the Tuskegee Airmen

There are stories which nations sometimes misplace — not by accident, but by design. Stories that make the gatekeepers of memory uncomfortable, that rattle the very hinges of prejudice, that refuse to be filed quietly away in the footnotes where some would prefer they reside. Yet history, though sometimes silenced, has a way of speaking again. It rises. It insists. It finds its voice in the most unexpected places — in the fading photograph of a young man in a flight suit, in the testimony of a bomber crew who swore they owed their lives to angels with crimson tails, in the tears of a grandfather who never spoke of the war but wept without explanation every time he heard a propeller engine overhead.

And so it is with the Tuskegee Airmen — the Black pilots and ground crews, the navigators and mechanics, the officers and enlisted men who, in the face of doubt, disdain, and deliberate obstruction, became not merely good, but great. Not merely competent, but legendary. Not merely soldiers, but symbols of something America claimed to believe in but had not yet earned the right to call its own.

They proved to the world, and to America herself, that courage cannot be bound by color, nor excellence diminished by hatred. They proved it not with words but with altitude — with throttle and rudder pedal and the cold mathematics of aerial combat. They proved it in the skies over North Africa and the Mediterranean, over Sicily and Southern Europe, with their distinctive crimson tails announcing their presence to friend and enemy alike. And the announcement was this: we are here, we have always been here, and you will not forget us.

The World They Were Born Into

To understand the Tuskegee Airmen, you must first understand the America that tried to tell them they could not fly.

It was an America that had given Black men the vote in 1870 and then spent the next seventy years finding ways to take it back. An America where a Black man could be lynched for looking at a white woman the wrong way, where the Supreme Court had declared segregation the law of the land, where Black citizens paid taxes to fund schools and libraries and public facilities they were forbidden to enter. It was an America at war with fascism abroad while practicing a quieter but no less vicious form of it at home.

The military reflected this America faithfully and completely. The armed forces were segregated by law and by culture. Black men had served in every American war — in the Revolution, in the Civil War where nearly 200,000

Black soldiers fought for the Union, in the Spanish-American War where the Buffalo Soldiers earned their reputation, in World War I where the Harlem Hellfighters fought under French command because American generals refused to integrate their units. In every war, Black men had served with distinction. In every war, their service had been minimized, dismissed, or erased from the official record.

By 1940, as war gathered on the horizon and America began to rearm, the Army Air Corps — the most elite, most technologically advanced branch of the military — maintained a simple and explicit policy: no Black pilots.

The reasoning, delivered with the confidence of those who have never bothered to question their own assumptions, was biological. Military officials cited studies — fraudulent, racist studies, though they did not call them that — claiming that Black men lacked the reflexes, the spatial reasoning, the emotional stability required for aerial combat. One Army report stated flatly that the Negro was fit for labor and support roles but constitutionally unsuited for positions requiring quick thinking and independent judgment.

This was not fringe thinking. This was official policy. This was science, as far as they were concerned.

And into this America, young Black men came forward and said: "we want to fly".

They came from everywhere. From the cities of the North — Chicago, Detroit, New York — where Black families had migrated during the Great Migration, trading the open terrorism of the South for the subtler but no less real discrimination of the North. From the colleges and universities of the South — Howard, Tuskegee, Morehouse — where Black scholars and professionals were being trained in defiance of every obstacle the nation placed before them. From small towns and large families and churches that told them every Sunday that they were made in the image of God and had no business believing anyone who said otherwise.

They came with college degrees and aviation experience and boundless ambition. They came knowing they would face resistance. They came anyway.

Benjamin O. Davis Jr. came from a military family — his father was Benjamin O. Davis Sr., who would become the first Black general in the United States Army. Young Benjamin had graduated from West Point in 1936, one of only a handful of Black graduates in the academy's history.

His four years there had been a study in deliberate cruelty — his white classmates had imposed a "silencing" on him, refusing to speak to him, eat with him, or room with him for the entirety of his time at the academy. He had endured it without complaint and graduated 35th in his class of 276. When he applied for the Army Air Corps, he was rejected. The Air Corps did not accept Black pilots.

Yancey Williams came from Washington, D.C., a college graduate who had taken flying lessons at his own expense.

He applied to the Army Air Corps and was rejected. He filed a lawsuit. The lawsuit, combined with pressure from civil rights organizations including the NAACP, and the political reality that Black voters in northern cities were becoming an important constituency, forced the Roosevelt administration's hand.

In 1941, the Army announced the formation of the 99th Pursuit Squadron — a segregated all-Black unit that would be trained at Tuskegee Army Air Field in Alabama. The announcement was made with minimal enthusiasm. Many within the military expected and privately hoped the experiment would fail. They chose Tuskegee because it was in Alabama — deep in the heart of Jim Crow country — perhaps calculating that the hostile environment would discourage the most determined applicants.

They miscalculated.

Tuskegee, Alabama

The men who arrived at Tuskegee Army Air Field found a landscape of contradiction. They were training to defend a democracy that did not fully include them, in a state that actively worked to exclude them from civic life. They trained on military equipment while being refused service at the lunch counters of nearby towns. They wore the uniform of the United States Army while being required to use separate facilities from their white counterparts. Off base, they were addressed without honorific, as if the rank on their collar meant nothing.

On base, they flew.

The training was rigorous, designed to be rigorous, designed perhaps to find the breaking point. They flew in heat that shimmered off the Alabama tarmac and made the air above it ripple and dance. They flew in conditions that would have washed out less determined men. They flew knowing that every mistake would be taken as proof of the thesis their enemies had already written — that Black men could not do this, should not be allowed to do this, were fundamentally unequal to this task.

They flew and they did not fail.

Captain Daniel "Chappie" James, who would later become the first Black four-star general in American history, trained at Tuskegee. He spoke of those days with a clarity that cut through sentiment: "We knew what we were doing. We weren't just learning to fly airplanes. We were flying against an idea. The idea that we were less."

Charles "Buster" Hall became the first Tuskegee Airman to shoot down an enemy aircraft, on July 2, 1943, over Sicily.

When the news reached the men at Tuskegee, there was celebration — not merely for the victory, but for what it meant. The enemy plane falling from the sky was not just an enemy plane. It was a lie falling from the sky.

The Red Tails

They were assigned to escort duty — protecting the heavy bombers that crossed into enemy territory on strategic missions over the heart of Nazi-occupied Europe. This was dangerous work of the highest order. The bombers were slow, massive, and incapable of defending themselves against the fast and maneuverable German fighters that rose to meet them. The fighter escorts were their only protection. And the fighter escorts, in the brutal attrition of aerial warfare, had developed a habit of abandoning the bombers they were assigned to protect in order to chase German fighters — chasing glory, chasing kill counts, leaving the bombers to fend for themselves.

The Tuskegee Airmen made a decision. They would not leave their bombers.

This decision, as much as their skill and courage, defined their reputation. The bomber crews began to request them specifically. Word traveled through the air groups: "f the Red Tails are with you, you will come home". They were not simply good fighter pilots. They were the most reliable escorts in the theater of war. In a world where reliability could mean the difference between your crew surviving or dying, they became beloved. They became, in the truest sense of the word - guardian angels.

By the end of the war, the 332nd Fighter Group — the unit that grew from the original 99th Pursuit Squadron — had flown more than 15,000 individual sorties. They had destroyed or damaged more than 400 enemy aircraft. They had sunk a destroyer — an extraordinary achievement for a fighter group — and destroyed hundreds of ground targets. They had earned more than 150 Distinguished Flying Crosses, and numerous other decorations. And perhaps most remarkably, they had never lost a bomber under their escort to enemy fighters.

Not one.

In the entire history of the air war over Europe, no other escort fighter group could make that claim.

The Men Behind the Men

But to speak only of the pilots is to speak only of the spire of the cathedral and forget the foundation. The Tuskegee Airmen were not only pilots. They were a community, a collective achievement, a demonstration of what Black excellence looks like when it is allowed to build on itself.

The mechanics who kept the aircraft flying worked with a devotion that went beyond duty. These were men who understood that the plane they were servicing would carry a brother, a friend, a man they had trained alongside, eaten with and joined in worship. Every bolt they tightened was tightened with that knowledge. One crew chief spoke of his work in terms that transcended the mechanical: "I knew that if I missed something, someone was going to die. Not someone. Someone I knew. Someone who trusted me. So I never missed anything."

The navigators plotted courses over hostile territory with instruments that were sometimes outdated, in conditions that were always dangerous, knowing that a mistake could send an entire mission into disaster. The intelligence officers analyzed reconnaissance photographs and briefed the pilots on what to expect. The support staff — cooks, clerks, drivers, medical personnel — maintained the infrastructure that made the flying possible.

And behind all of them, almost literally, stood the institution of Tuskegee University itself, and its leader, Dr.

Frederick Douglass Patterson, who had lobbied the government to allow Black men to train there, who had staked the reputation of his institution on the proposition that these men could fly and fight and win. He had been right.

Colonel Davis Leads

Benjamin O. Davis Jr. led the 332nd Fighter Group with a command presence that inspired both admiration and something close to awe. He was demanding, precise, and utterly without self-pity. He had been silenced for four years at West Point and had responded by graduating near the top of his class. He had been rejected by the Air Corps and had responded by becoming one of its finest officers.

He had been denied and dismissed and condescended to at every turn, and he had responded every time the same way — with performance so excellent that denial became impossible to sustain.

His men followed him not merely because of his rank but because of what he represented: the proposition, proven by his very existence, that discipline and excellence were not the property of any race, that leadership was not a genetic inheritance, that the barriers placed before them were constructed of prejudice and not of truth.

When Davis returned to Washington to testify before the War Department about the performance of his men, he spoke with a directness that must have been startling in the halls of military power: "The Tuskegee Airmen have demonstrated conclusively that the colored American, given adequate training, equipment, and opportunity, can perform any task that is asked of him in the war effort." He was not boasting. He was reporting facts. The facts were irrefutable.

The Return Home

And then they came home.

They came home to an America that had not changed as much as they had hoped. They came home as decorated war heroes and were told to move to the back of the bus.

They came home with Distinguished Flying Crosses and Purple Hearts and were addressed without their rank by men who had never served a day.

Some of them came home and fought this America with the same determination they had brought to the skies over Europe. They became lawyers and doctors and engineers and educators. They became civil rights activists. They marched and organized and voted and ran for office. The discipline and courage that had made them warriors made them, in peacetime, something equally powerful — citizens who refused to accept the gap between what America claimed to be and what it actually was.

Others came home and said little about what they had done and what they had seen. They built lives and raised children and went to church and held their memories privately, like a light kept burning in a room that others rarely entered.

But the world had changed, even if America was slow to follow. In 1948, three years after the war ended, President Harry Truman signed Executive Order 9981, desegregating the United States Armed Forces. The order was not solely the result of the Tuskegee Airmen's service — other forces were at work as well — but no honest accounting of that order's origins can omit the fact that these men had made the argument for integration with their performance. They had not argued in words. They had argued in altitude, in aerial victories, in bombers brought safely home. They had argued in the testimony of white bomber crews who had flown beneath their protection and wanted everyone to know it.

They had won the argument.

The Erasure and the Remembering

For decades after the war, the story of the Tuskegee Airmen existed primarily in the memories of the men themselves, in the archives of historically Black colleges and universities, in the oral traditions of Black families where grandfathers told their grandchildren about men who flew. The mainstream telling of World War II — the movies, the textbooks, the monuments — largely omitted them. Their portraits did not hang on the walls of military academies. Their names did not appear in the indexes of standard histories.

This was not accidental. The same machinery of erasure that had operated against Black achievement throughout American history operated here. If the story of the Tuskegee Airmen became widely known and celebrated, it would complicate the narrative of Black inferiority that had justified segregation, discrimination, and the daily denial of Black humanity. Better, from the perspective of that machinery, to let the story fade.

It did not fade.

The men themselves formed the Tuskegee Airmen organization and began telling their own story — in schools and community centers and churches and conference rooms, wherever anyone would listen.

Researchers and historians began to document what had been omitted. Eventually the story broke through into the mainstream — into documentaries, into a major motion picture, into Congressional Gold Medals presented to the surviving Airmen by President George W. Bush in 2007.

The surviving Airmen who attended that ceremony — old men by then, most of them in their eighties and nineties, some in wheelchairs — wept. Not from sentiment alone but from something more complex: the long-delayed recognition of a truth they had always known, finally spoken aloud in the halls of power.

And now, in our own time, there are those who would undo this recognition — who would remove the portraits of the Tuskegee Airmen from the walls where they had finally been hung, who would strike their story from academic syllabi, websites and official histories - who would return them to the footnotes where they had been relegated for so long.

We will not allow it.

This chapter is our refusal. The Cathedral our stand. Here and now we write their name - not in pencil but in stone:

Benjamin O. Davis Jr. Charles "Buster" Hall. Daniel "Chappie" James. Lee Archer. Roscoe Brown. Herbert Carter. William Campbell. Clarence "Lucky" Lester, who shot down three enemy aircraft in a single mission.

Alexander Jefferson, who survived being shot down and imprisoned in a German POW camp. Hiram Mann. Harry Stewart.

And the hundreds of others — pilots, navigators, bombardiers, mechanics, crew chiefs, intelligence officers, administrators — whose names fill the rosters of the 99th Pursuit Squadron and the 332nd Fighter Group and the 477th Bombardment Group, the full community of men who together made history so undeniable that even those determined to forget it could not entirely succeed.

Their Legacy, Our Inheritance

The legacy of the Tuskegee Airmen extends beyond military history; it proves what's possible when people defy a verdict rooted in falsehood. It is irrefutable evidence that the barriers placed were never about ability, but fear - fear of what true Black excellence would reveal.

And in revealing that excellence they soared. They soared above North Africa, the Mediterranean and Southern Europe. They soared above the doubts of generals and the prejudices of policy. They soared above an America that had told them explicitly and repeatedly, that there were heights Black ambition would never reach.

The Tuskegee Airmen did not merely reach those heights.

They flew past them.

CHAPTER TWO

The Pen Was Never Silent

A Tribute to Black Writers

There is a particular kind of violence that leaves no visible wound. It does not announce itself with chains or whips or the crack of a rifle. It operates quietly, systematically, with the patience of institutions that have centuries to accomplish their work. It is the violence of erasure — the deliberate removal of a people from the record of human achievement, the calculated theft not of property or liberty - but of story.

To steal a people's story is to steal something more fundamental than land or labor. Land can be reclaimed.

Labor can be compensated - however inadequately. But story — the narrative of who you are and where you come from and what you have made and what you are capable of making — story is the architecture of the self. Destroy it and you do not merely impoverish a people. You convince them, and those around them, that there is nothing there to impoverish.

This is what the suppressors of Black literary achievement understood, whether consciously or by instinct. This is why literacy was criminalized under slavery. This is why Black authors were dismissed, ignored, and condescended to for generations. This is why the canon of American literature was constructed with such deliberate narrowness, as though the vast richness of Black literary tradition did not exist, or existed only as a curiosity, a footnote, an asterisk beside the main text of civilization.

They were wrong, and the writers themselves proved it — not by arguing the point but by writing. By writing with such force, beauty and truth that the argument became unnecessary. The work itself was the argument. The work itself was the victory.

But we must begin before the page, before the ink, before the very concept of written literature existed in the Western sense. We must begin with the griot.

In the civilizations of West Africa — in the great kingdoms of Mali and Songhai and the Wolof states of what is now Senegal and Gambia — the griot was the keeper of culture.

Not merely a storyteller, though storytelling was central to the work. The griot was historian, genealogist, diplomat, musician, and poet combined into a single indispensable office. A griot could stand before a king and recite the lineage of his family going back twenty, thirty, forty generations. A griot could resolve disputes by recalling precedents that had been established before any living person was born. A griot carried, in memory, what modern civilization stores in libraries.

This was not primitive. This was sophisticated. This was a technology of memory that served cultures that chose oral transmission not because they lacked the capacity for writing but because they understood, perhaps better than literate cultures, that language lives in the breath, in the body, in the relationship between speaker and listener.

The griot's art required not only a prodigious memory but a mastery of performance — of rhythm and tone and the ability to make history feel immediate and present, to make the dead speak again.

When our ancestors were taken from Africa in the holds of ships, the griots among them could not bring their libraries. But they brought something that no ship's hold could contain: the tradition. The understanding that story is survival. The conviction that memory is resistance. The knowledge that as long as the people keep telling, the people keep living.

It is from this root that Black American literature grows.

Not from imitation of European models — though Black writers engaged brilliantly with those models and transformed them — but from something older and deeper.

From the understanding, written into the very genes of the tradition, that to speak is to survive, and to write is to endure.

Phillis Wheatley and the First Defiance

In 1773, a young woman named Phillis Wheatley published a book of poems in London. She was twenty years old. She had been taken from West Africa — from what is now

Senegal or Gambia, scholars believe — when she was approximately seven or eight years old, small enough that she had lost her front teeth, which is how the record describes her at the time of her purchase by John Wheatley of Boston. She had been purchased as a household servant.

She learned to read within sixteen months of her arrival.

Within a few years she was reading Latin and Greek and the English poets — Pope, Milton, the classical authors.

She began writing poetry. By the time she was in her mid- teens she was corresponding with some of the most prominent figures of the colonial era.

When she sought to publish her poems, the male literary establishment of Boston convened a tribunal — eighteen prominent men, including John Hancock — to determine whether she, an enslaved African woman, could actually have written what she claimed to have written. They questioned her extensively. They concluded, apparently to their own surprise, that she had.

The book was published. It was the first book of poetry published by an African American and one of the first published by an American woman of any background. It was read in Europe and America. Voltaire mentioned it.

George Washington, to whom she had written a poem, invited her to visit him, and she did.

She died at thirty-one, in poverty, having been freed after her enslaver's death and having outlived the children she bore. Her husband was imprisoned for debt. She died alone. The world moved on.

But the poems remained.

And what the poems said — this is what matters — was that the mind behind them was fully human, fully capable, fully present. The poems said, in the formal cadences of eighteenth-century verse, what would need to be said again and again in the centuries that followed: we are here, we think, we feel, we create, and no circumstance of our enslavement can alter the fundamental truth of our humanity.

She wrote this in 1773. She wrote it before there was a United States of America. She wrote it before the word "abolitionist" had entered common usage. She wrote it alone, in a city that had purchased her like furniture, and she wrote it so well that the men who gathered to decide whether she was capable of writing had to admit, however reluctantly, that she was.

This was the first defiance. It would not be the last.

Frederick Douglass and the Autobiography as Weapon

In 1845, a man named Frederick Douglass published the story of his life. He had been born into slavery in Maryland, had taught himself to read with the help of his enslaver's wife and then in secret after she was forbidden to continue his education, had escaped north in 1838, and had become one of the most powerful voices of the abolitionist movement. His speaking had drawn enormous crowds and had moved many to tears and many to action.

But there were always those who doubted — who said that no man who spoke and carried himself as Douglass did could possibly have been enslaved, that his story must be fabricated, that no slave could have such command of language and argument.

So he wrote it down. He wrote the Narrative of the Life of Frederick Douglass, An American Slave, Written by Himself — including those last four words in the title deliberately, defiantly. He wrote the names of his enslavers and the places where they had held him and the specific acts of violence and degradation he had witnessed and endured. He wrote it knowing that in doing so he risked capture and re-enslavement under the Fugitive Slave Act.

He wrote it anyway.

The book sold 30,000 copies in its first five years. It was translated into French and Dutch. It was read throughout the antislavery movement in Europe and America. It made the abstract argument for abolition concrete and human — it gave the system of slavery a face, and it gave the enslaved a voice that was impossible to dismiss as inarticulate or inferior.

Douglass understood what he was doing. He wrote later: "Knowledge makes a man unfit to be a slave." But the full meaning of that sentence cuts deeper than it might first appear. He was not saying merely that educated people resist oppression more effectively, though that is also true.

He was saying something about the nature of slavery itself — that it required, for its operation, the suppression of the knowledge of the enslaved. That the entire system depended on keeping Black people from knowing their own worth, their own history, their own capacity. And that the moment they knew — the moment they could read and write and tell their own stories — the system's foundations began to crack.

He wrote himself free. Not legally — the law still held him.

But in the deeper sense that matters more: he wrote himself into the record of humanity as a full and equal participant. He made his erasure impossible.

This is what every Black writer who came after him was doing, consciously or not. Writing against erasure. Writing themselves and their people into the record. Writing, as an act of profound resistance, the simple and radical truth: we are here.

The Harlem Renaissance: A People Discovers Its Voice

In the years following the First World War, something extraordinary happened in a neighborhood in upper Manhattan. African Americans had been migrating north for decades — fleeing the terrorism of the South, seeking work in the industrial cities of the North, carrying with them their music and their food and their faith and their stories. And in Harlem, New York, they gathered in such numbers and with such energy that something unprecedented became possible: a Black cultural community of sufficient density and vitality to sustain a literary movement.

The Harlem Renaissance, as it came to be called, was more than a literary movement. It was a philosophical reckoning. It was a community of artists and intellectuals deciding, together and separately and in the beautiful collision of their individual visions, what it meant to be Black in America — not as a problem to be solved or a burden to be managed, but as an identity to be celebrated, explored, complicated, and claimed.

Langston Hughes was its most beloved poet, and also its most democratic one. Where others in the movement sometimes aspired to the formal heights of European literature, Hughes went down — down to the streets and the jazz clubs and the church pews and the kitchens, to the rhythms of Black vernacular speech and Black music. He wrote poems that swung like jazz and ached like the blues.

He wrote "The Negro Speaks of Rivers" at seventeen years old, on a train crossing the Mississippi, and produced in a single poem a meditation on Black history and identity that moves readers to tears a century later. He wrote "I, Too, Sing America" — its twelve lines containing an entire argument about belonging and dignity and the long arc of justice that is still being contested today.

He was not the only one.

Zora Neale Hurston was a novelist and anthropologist from Eatonville, Florida — the first incorporated all-Black town in America — and she brought to her work an intimacy with Black Southern culture that was entirely her own. Her novel Their Eyes Were Watching God, published in 1937, is one of the greatest American novels ever written. It is the story of a Black woman's inner life — her desires, her growth, her voice — rendered with a lyricism that has never been equaled. It was criticized by some of her contemporaries, including Richard Wright, for its perceived lack of political engagement. History has not been kind to that criticism. What Hurston understood, and what the passage of time has confirmed, is that the fullest act of resistance is not always the most explicitly political one. Sometimes the most radical thing you can do is insist on the full complexity and beauty of a Black woman's interior world — to say: she is not a symbol, not a problem, not a cause. She is a person. Here is what she thinks and feels and desires and fears. Here is her voice, exact and irreplaceable, and it is literature.

Claude McKay wrote "If We Must Die," a sonnet composed in 1919 in response to the wave of anti-Black violence that swept America that summer — what historians would call the Red Summer, when white mobs attacked Black communities in dozens of American cities. The sonnet does not mention race explicitly. It speaks of men facing overwhelming odds and choosing to die fighting rather than to die "like hogs / Hunted and penned in an inglorious spot." It was read aloud in the British Parliament during the Second World War, cited by Winston Churchill as an example of the defiant spirit needed to resist fascism. Churchill did not mention its origins. The spirit was Black. The defiance was

Black. The words were Black. The world used them and forgot where they came from. We remember.

Countee Cullen, James Weldon Johnson, Nella Larsen, Jean Toomer, Arna Bontemps — each of them, in their own way, was doing what the griot had always done: holding the mirror up to a people and saying, look, this is who you are, this is what you have made, this is what you are capable of. The mirror they held up showed not the diminished, dehumanized image that white America projected onto Black people, but the full and complicated and beautiful truth.

The Midcentury Giants

The Harlem Renaissance planted seeds that bloomed in the middle decades of the twentieth century with a force that shook the foundations of American culture and conscience.

Richard Wright's Native Son, published in 1940, was a detonation. It told the story of Bigger Thomas, a young Black man in Chicago whose life is shaped at every turn by the violence of racism — not the violence of individual racists alone, but the systemic, ambient violence of a society that has made him, through poverty and exclusion and the daily message of his own worthlessness, into something dangerous. Wright did not flinch. He did not offer the comfortable narrative of the exceptional Negro who triumphs over adversity. He offered something harder and more honest: the portrait of what happens when a human being is systematically denied his humanity. The book sold 250,000 copies in its first three weeks. It forced a conversation about race that America did not want to have.

Ralph Ellison published Invisible Man in 1952 and won the National Book Award, becoming the first African American to do so. The novel's opening sentence — "I am an invisible man" — announces its central metaphor and its central truth: that American society's refusal to see Black people as fully human renders them, in a profound sense, invisible. Not literally unseen, but unseen in the way that matters — their inner lives, their complexity, their full humanity, passed over and unacknowledged. The novel is a masterpiece of American literature, full stop, not with the asterisk that once marked Black achievement in white critical consciousness but without qualification or caveat.

James Baldwin was perhaps the most incandescent prose writer America produced in the twentieth century, of any background. His essays — collected in Notes of a Native Son, The Fire Next Time, Nobody Knows My Name — are exercises in a particular kind of intellectual and moral courage: the courage to look directly at the most painful truths and describe them with absolute precision, without the comfort of euphemism, without the false mercy of looking away. He wrote to white America: "I know what the world has done to my brother and how narrowly he has survived it, and I know which of us has been mad and which of us has been sane." He wrote this in 1963, in The Fire Next Time, and the America he described in those pages is recognizable today — which tells us something about how much has changed, and how much has not.

Baldwin lived much of his adult life in France, an expatriate by necessity — the weight of American racism was too much to carry and still write. From Paris and Istanbul and

Saint-Paul-de-Vence he wrote about America with the clarity that distance provides and the intimacy that love — for his people, for the country that had failed them — makes possible. He never stopped believing that America could be better. He never stopped being honest about how far it had to go.

Gwendolyn Brooks became, in 1950, the first African American to win the Pulitzer Prize, for her collection Annie Allen. She wrote with a formal precision that was also, always, deeply rooted in the lives of ordinary Black people — in the kitchens and barbershops and pool halls and churches of Chicago's South Side, where she spent her life.

Her poem "We Real Cool" is seven lines long and contains more truth about youth and mortality and the particular vulnerability of young Black men than most novels manage in three hundred pages. She taught. She mentored. She stayed in Chicago when she could have gone anywhere. She understood that art is not made in isolation from the community that produces it.

The Nobel Laureates

In 1993, Toni Morrison stood before the Swedish Academy and delivered a Nobel lecture that is itself one of the masterpieces of American prose. She spoke of language — of the responsibility of writers to language, and of language's capacity to liberate or oppress. She spoke of the "dead language" that serves power — "Sexist language, racist language, theistic language — all are typical of the policing languages of mastery, and cannot, do not permit new knowledge or encourage the mutual exchange of ideas." And she spoke of the alternative: language "that moves away from its own excesses and needs, a language that cherishes what it is not — 'the speech of animals,' those creatures who might better know 'what language is, what it wants, what it requires.'"

She was, by that point, the author of The Bluest Eye, Sula, Song of Solomon, Tar Baby, Beloved, Jazz, and Paradise — a body of work that constitutes one of the great achievements in the history of American literature.

Beloved, published in 1987, is based on the true story of Margaret Garner, a formerly enslaved woman who killed her daughter rather than see her returned to slavery. It confronts, with unsparing directness, the psychic devastation of slavery — what it did to the bodies and minds and souls of those who survived it and those who did not. It is a ghost story and a love story and a history lesson and a meditation on memory and trauma, all at once, written in prose of such beauty that readers describe the experience of it as physical.

Morrison had grown up in Lorain, Ohio, the daughter of working-class parents who had migrated from Georgia and Alabama. She became an editor at Random House, where she championed the work of other Black writers. She taught at Princeton. She wrote eleven novels and received every major literary honor her country could bestow. And she remained, always, committed to the truth that Black life — in its fullness, its complexity, its beauty and its pain — was the most worthy subject for literature she could imagine.

Maya Angelou wrote I Know Why the Caged Bird Sings in 1969 and inaugurated a tradition of Black women's autobiography that transformed American letters. The book told the story of her childhood in Stamps, Arkansas — the racism, the violence, the beauty, the survival, the triumph of a spirit that refused, against all logic and all evidence, to be broken. She recited "On the Pulse of Morning" at Bill Clinton's inauguration in 1993, the first poet to read at a presidential inauguration since Robert Frost in 1961. She stood before the nation and spoke of welcome and inclusion and the long, difficult, necessary work of becoming what America had always claimed to be.

The Contemporary Voices

The tradition continues, as traditions do — not in a straight line but in the organic, branching way of living things, constantly finding new forms for the same ancient impulse.

Ta-Nehisi Coates brought to the question of race in America a ferocity of intellect and a willingness to follow the argument wherever it leads that recalled Baldwin at his most fearless. His book Between the World and Me,

written as a letter to his teenage son, meditates on Black bodies in America — their vulnerability, their beauty, the particular terror of raising a Black child in a country that has never fully valued Black life. It is not a comfortable book. It is not meant to be. It is meant to be honest, and it is.

Jesmyn Ward writes of the Mississippi Gulf Coast with the intimacy of someone who knows it in her bones — its beauty, its poverty, its particular history of racial violence, its people. Her novels Salvage the Bones and Sing, Unburied, Sing are works of profound compassion and formal brilliance. She has won the National Book Award twice, a distinction shared by very few American writers.

Amanda Gorman stepped to the microphone at Joseph Biden's inauguration on January 20, 2021, and did what poets rarely get the chance to do in American public life: she made the nation stop and listen. She was twenty-two years old. She had grown up in Los Angeles, had been diagnosed with a speech impediment as a child, had turned her love of language into a weapon of hope. She read "The Hill We Climb," and the words she read were not merely beautiful — though they were beautiful — they were necessary. They named what the moment required: "We will not march back to what was, but move to what shall be — a country that is bruised but whole, benevolent but bold, fierce and free." A country, she said, that needed to keep climbing.

She was right. And she was Black, and young, and female, and brilliant, and she stood there in front of the nation and the world and recited her own words — words she had written — and the moment was one of those rare ones in which you can feel, almost physically, the weight of history pressing against the present.

Phillis Wheatley would have recognized it. So would Douglass. So would Hughes and Hurston and Baldwin and Morrison. The thread runs unbroken from the griot's fire to the inauguration platform — the same commitment, the same conviction, the same act of profound resistance:

We will tell our own story.

We will tell it in our own voice.

And we will tell it so well that you cannot look away.

The Unsung Voices

And then there are the ones the canon has not yet recognized. The poets who published chapbooks in church basements. The novelists whose manuscripts sit in university archives, waiting for a scholar who will understand what they were doing. The journalists and essayists and bloggers and spoken word artists who carry the tradition forward in forms that the gatekeepers of literature have been slow to acknowledge.

Every grandmother who sat her grandchildren down and told them about the old country, the old neighborhood, the people who came before — she was a griot. Every preacher who made the congregation feel the presence of the divine through the music of language — he was a griot. Every teacher who read poetry aloud to her students and made them feel, for the first time, that language could be a home — she was a griot.

The tradition is not only in the books. It is in the telling. It is in the insistence, passed from generation to generation, that our stories matter. That our voices are worth hearing.

That the literature we make is not a lesser literature, not a regional literature, not a special-interest literature, but a literature — full and serious and indispensable to the understanding of what it means to be human in this country and on this earth.

The First and the Final Word

Let it be declared, without qualification and without apology: Black writers have not merely contributed to American literature. They have, at crucial moments, been American literature — its conscience, its prophet, its most honest voice. When America needed to hear the truth about what it was doing and what it was failing to do, it was Black writers who told it. When the nation's self- deception grew too comfortable, it was Black writers who made it uncomfortable. When the story of American democracy needed to be completed — needed to include the voices of those it had excluded and the experiences of those it had tried to forget — it was Black writers who completed it.

They did not do this for gratitude. Most of them received very little. They did it because the story needed to be told, and they were the ones who could tell it, and they understood that to be entrusted with that telling was not a burden but a calling.

From Phillis Wheatley to Amanda Gorman. From Frederick Douglass to Ta-Nehisi Coates. From Zora Neale Hurston to Jesmyn Ward. From Langston Hughes to Kendrick Lamar — because yes, the tradition of Black oral poetry did not stop at the page; it kept going, into the microphone, into the recording studio, into the speaker at full volume on a summer evening.

The thread is unbroken.

The voice is unsilenced.

The pen was never silent.

Not for them.

Not for us.

And this is the final word: that no removal from syllabi, no closed library, no burned book shall undo this truth. The words are written. The books exist. The tradition lives — in libraries and living rooms and churches and classrooms and the memories of every person who has ever read a line by a Black writer and felt, in the marrow of their bones, the shock of recognition.

We wrote for our country. We wrote for its soul.

And we shall write still.

CHAPTER THREE

The Mind Was Never Shackled

A Tribute to Black Scientists and Inventors

There is a particular pleasure that power takes in declaring certain minds unfit for certain work. It requires no evidence, produces its own, and is self-confirming in the most convenient way: deny access, observe absence, cite absence as proof of incapacity. The circle is complete and the lie is dressed as logic.

For centuries, this logic was applied to Black intellectual life with the full force of law and institution. Black people were barred from universities and laboratories and patent offices and professional societies. When they managed, despite these barriers, to produce work of genuine scientific merit, that work was minimized, misattributed, or stolen outright. And when their exclusion produced the absence of representation that the system had designed it to produce, that absence was cited as evidence that they had never belonged there in the first place.

It was, in the truest sense, a lie that ate itself — surviving only because the people who told it controlled the institutions that might have corrected it.

But the mind, as it turns out, does not require permission to work.

Before the Academy, There Was Knowledge

We must begin again before the Western academy, because the story of Black scientific achievement does not begin with the first Black student admitted to a segregated university. It begins in Africa, where the foundations of mathematics, astronomy, medicine, and engineering were laid thousands of years before Europe had institutions in which to teach them.

The ancient Egyptians — whose civilization was African, whatever centuries of miseducation have tried to suggest otherwise — developed a mathematical system sophisticated enough to plan and execute the construction of the pyramids, structures so precisely engineered that modern architects continue to study them with something close to reverence. The Great Pyramid of Giza is aligned with the cardinal directions with an accuracy that varies by less than one-tenth of a degree. Its base is level to within two centimeters across a footprint that covers more than thirteen acres. This was not accomplished by accident.

This was accomplished by people who understood geometry, astronomy, surveying, and engineering at a level that no amount of condescension can diminish.

The scholars of Timbuktu, in medieval Mali, maintained a university at which tens of thousands of students studied mathematics, astronomy, medicine, law, and theology. The Sankore Mosque housed a library of between 400,000 and 700,000 manuscripts — one of the largest collections of written knowledge in the medieval world. These were not primitive texts. They were treatises on surgery, on the movement of celestial bodies, on the philosophical foundations of mathematics.

This is where we begin. Not with the first Black man admitted to MIT. But with the civilization that invented the mathematics MIT teaches.

Benjamin Banneker: The First Defiance of American Science

In 1791, a self-educated free Black man named Benjamin Banneker wrote a letter to Thomas Jefferson. Jefferson had recently written, in his Notes on the State of Virginia, that Black people were "inferior to the whites in the endowments both of body and mind." Banneker, who had taught himself mathematics and astronomy from borrowed books, who had built a functioning clock from scratch after studying a pocket watch, who had calculated ephemerides — the complex astronomical tables used to create almanacs — of sufficient accuracy that they were published and sold throughout the mid-Atlantic states, wrote to Jefferson with restrained but devastating precision.

He enclosed a copy of his almanac. He asked Jefferson to reconcile his stated beliefs about Black inferiority with the evidence enclosed. He wrote: "I apprehend you will embrace every opportunity to eradicate that train of absurd and false ideas and opinions which so generally prevails with respect to us."

Jefferson wrote back, acknowledged the almanac, expressed his hopes that Banneker's example would disprove the prejudices of the age. Then he continued to enslave people.

But Banneker had made his point. The almanac existed.

The calculations were accurate. The mind behind them was unambiguously brilliant. No assertion of inferiority could survive direct contact with the fact of Benjamin Banneker.

He continued publishing his almanacs until 1797. He surveyed the boundaries of what would become the District of Columbia — the capital city of the nation that considered him less than fully human — and his calculations were accurate. He died in 1806. His farmhouse burned to the ground on the day of his funeral, destroying most of his papers and instruments.

The almanacs survived.

George Washington Carver: The Poet of the Laboratory

There is a story — possibly apocryphal but spiritually true — that George Washington Carver would go into his laboratory early in the morning, before anyone else arrived, and sit quietly with the plants and soils and seeds he was studying, as if in conversation with them. He spoke of his scientific practice in the language of listening, of attention, of respect for the intelligence embedded in creation. "I love to think of nature as an unlimited broadcasting station," he said, "through which God speaks to us every hour, if we will only tune in."

This might sound like sentiment. It was, in fact, methodology.

Carver was born into slavery in Missouri around 1864 — the exact date is unknown, records of enslaved people's births being considered unnecessary — and was kidnapped as an infant along with his mother by night raiders. His mother was never recovered. He was ransomed back to his enslaver for a horse. He grew up as the only Black student in a series of schools, walking miles to reach them, washing and pressing his single set of clothes each night so he could present himself the next morning with dignity.

He earned a bachelor's degree and then a master's degree in botany from Iowa State University — the first African American to do either — and was asked to join the faculty.

He declined, accepting instead an offer from Booker T. Washington to come to Tuskegee Institute and work with the farmers of the Black Belt South, who were locked in a cycle of poverty enforced by their dependence on cotton, a crop that depleted the soil and left them at the mercy of price fluctuations they could not control.

Carver's approach to this problem was scientific and also revolutionary. He analyzed the soil. He studied the crops that restored what cotton depleted. He developed alternative crops — peanuts and sweet potatoes and soybeans — that could break the cycle. And then, anticipating the objection that farmers couldn't eat peanuts if there was no market for them, he invented the market. He developed more than 300 products derived from the peanut — paints, stains, cosmetics, medicines, adhesives, plastics — and more than 100 from the sweet potato. He did not patent most of these inventions. He believed that knowledge belonged to everyone.

He testified before Congress in 1921 on behalf of peanut tariffs, and his performance was so extraordinary — his knowledge so deep, his presentation so engaging — that the hostile committee chairman who had given him ten minutes ultimately gave him unlimited time. He received a standing ovation.

He was paid $1,500 a year at Tuskegee. Thomas Edison offered him a salary reported to be $100,000 a year and the resources of his laboratory. Carver declined. He stayed at Tuskegee. He stayed with his people.

When he died in 1943, the tributes were global. Franklin Roosevelt called him "an inspiration to his race and to the nation." Henry Ford, who had become his friend, wept.

But perhaps the most fitting tribute came from the farmers of the Alabama Black Belt, whose soil he had healed and whose economic possibilities he had transformed, one peanut at a time.

Charles Drew and the Blood That Saved the World

In the summer of 1940, as the German air force was bombing Britain into rubble and the casualty lists were growing faster than the hospitals could manage them, a young Black surgeon named Charles Drew was completing research that would save hundreds of thousands of lives — research into blood plasma and how it could be stored and transported and used to sustain injured soldiers until more definitive treatment was possible.

Drew had grown up in Washington, D.C., had excelled at every academic challenge presented to him, had attended Amherst College and McGill University medical school and Columbia University, where he became the first African American to earn a Doctor of Science degree. He was, by the time he completed his plasma research, one of the leading authorities in the world on blood banking.

The British government asked him to establish a blood bank program for their military. He designed it. He ran it.

It worked. Thousands of wounded soldiers survived who would otherwise have died.

The American military then asked him to establish a similar program for the United States. He agreed. He became director of the first large-scale American blood bank.

And then the American Red Cross, yielding to pressure from racists within the military establishment, announced that blood would be segregated — that blood donated by Black Americans would be stored separately from blood donated by white Americans and would not be given to white soldiers.

Drew publicly opposed this policy. He stated, clearly and correctly, that there was no scientific basis for it — that blood does not carry racial characteristics, that a Black man's blood would save a white man's life as surely as the reverse, that the policy was not medicine but bigotry dressed in medical language.

He was overruled. The policy was implemented.

He resigned.

He returned to Howard University, where he built one of the finest surgery departments in the country and trained an entire generation of Black surgeons. He died in 1950, in a car accident in North Carolina, and was taken to the nearest hospital, which was segregated. The legend — repeated for decades — that he was denied a blood transfusion because of his race and bled to death as a result has been disputed by historians who have examined the records; it appears he received treatment but his injuries were too severe. But the legend persisted because it felt true — because it captured something real about the way America treated its Black geniuses, even as it used their gifts.

His blood saved the world. America could not save the dignity of the man who showed it how.

Katherine Johnson: The Human Computer

On February 20, 1962, John Glenn climbed into the Friendship 7 capsule and prepared to become the first American to orbit the Earth. The computers at NASA had calculated his trajectory. Glenn was not entirely confident in the computers.

He asked for Katherine.

Katherine Johnson, a Black woman from White Sulphur Springs, West Virginia, was a mathematician at NASA — one of a group of Black women known informally as "computers," because they performed by hand the calculations that the early electronic computers were not yet fully trusted to perform. She had graduated from West Virginia State College at eighteen with degrees in mathematics and French, had been one of the first Black students admitted to West Virginia University's graduate program in mathematics, and had been doing the essential work of space travel while working in an office designated "colored computers" and using separate bathrooms from her white colleagues.

Glenn said: if the girl says the numbers are good, then I'm ready to go.

The girl verified the numbers. They were good. Glenn flew.

The mission succeeded.

Johnson's calculations were foundational to the Mercury program, to the Apollo program, to the mission that put men on the moon. She calculated the trajectory for Apollo 11. She worked on the Space Shuttle program and on plans for a mission to Mars. She received the Presidential Medal of Freedom in 2015, at the age of ninety-seven. A film was made about her and the other Black women who had performed this essential, invisible work — Hidden Figures, the title describing both the mathematical and the human reality.

She was not hidden because she lacked ability. She was hidden because a society committed to a lie about Black intellectual capacity could not afford to prominently acknowledge the people whose work made its greatest achievements possible.

The lie required hiding. The truth required finding.

We have found it.

Mae Jemison: Carrying the Ancestors to the Stars

On September 12, 1992, Mae Jemison floated weightless in the shuttle Endeavour, 190 miles above the surface of the Earth, and looked down at the planet that had told her, in a thousand ways large and small, that she did not belong in space.

She had known she wanted to be a scientist since she was a child in Chicago. She had told her kindergarten teacher she wanted to be a scientist. The teacher asked if she meant a nurse. She did not mean a nurse. She earned a degree in chemical engineering from Stanford and a medical degree from Cornell. She served as a Peace Corps medical officer in West Africa. She was selected by NASA in 1987 as one of fifteen candidates from more than 2,000 applicants.

When she floated in that shuttle, she was carrying more than herself. She was carrying every ancestor who had been told that the sky was the limit. She was carrying Mae Carol Jemison of Chicago, Illinois, who had looked up at the stars as a child and understood, with the absolute certainty of a mind that has recognized its own calling, that she would go there.

Before each mission, shuttle crew members are allowed to bring a small number of personal items. Jemison brought a poster from the Alvin Ailey American Dance Theater, a flag that had flown over the Organization of African Unity, and a photograph of Bessie Coleman — the first Black woman to earn a pilot's license, who had to go to France to earn it because no American flight school would accept her.

The ancestors were in the capsule. The ancestors reached the stars.

The Inventors Hidden in Plain Sight

The patent record of the United States contains thousands of inventions by Black Americans — though it contains far fewer than actually exist, because for much of American history, enslaved people could not hold patents, and free Black inventors often found their patents denied or their work appropriated.

Granville Woods, whom some called the "Black Edison," held more than 60 patents. His induction telegraph system, which allowed moving trains to communicate with stations, was purchased by Thomas Edison after Edison's attempts to develop a competing system failed. Woods developed improvements to electrical motors, to telephone systems, to brake systems for trains. He spent much of his professional life defending his patents against appropriation.

Lewis Howard Latimer drafted the patent drawings for Alexander Graham Bell's telephone. He developed an improved carbon filament for the incandescent light bulb that made Edison's invention commercially viable — the original filaments burned out quickly; Latimer's lasted much longer. He was one of the few Black members of the Edison Pioneers, the group of scientists and engineers who had worked directly with Edison.

Jan Ernst Matzeliger invented the lasting machine — a device that mechanically attached the upper part of a shoe to its sole, a process that had previously required skilled hand labor and took up to 80 hours per pair of shoes. His invention reduced the cost of shoes by fifty percent and made footwear affordable to working-class Americans. He died at thirty-seven of tuberculosis, his fortune not yet made, his invention already transforming an industry.

Lonnie Johnson, a NASA engineer who worked on the Galileo mission to Jupiter and the Cassini mission to Saturn, was tinkering at home one day with a pump he was building when he accidentally squirted a stream of water across the bathroom with impressive force and distance.

He spent the next several years developing that accident

into the Super Soaker water gun, which became one of the best-selling toys in history and made him wealthy enough to fund his engineering research company, where he continued developing energy storage technologies and thin-film solar cells.

He turned play into profit and profit into science. He took what gave children joy and used it to fund work that might give the planet a future. This is what Black inventors do: find the profound in the practical, the universal in the specific, the possibility in the overlooked and the dismissed.

The Future Is Ours to Invent

We stand at a moment when the fields that will determine the future of human civilization — artificial intelligence, genetic medicine, climate science, quantum computing, aerospace engineering — are fields in which Black representation remains far below what the talent and the need would justify. This is not because the talent is absent.

It is because the pipeline that leads to these fields — from elementary school science classes to university research positions to corporate and government laboratories — still carries, at every stage, the residue of centuries of exclusion.

But the talent is there. It has always been there. It was there in the fields of Tuskegee, where George Washington Carver listened to the soil. It was there in the segregated office at NASA, where Katherine Johnson calculated the numbers that sent men to the moon. It is there today, in every classroom where a Black child leans forward over a microscope or a circuit board or a coding interface and feels, in the recognition of their own aptitude, the voice of every ancestor who was told they could not do this and did it anyway.

Our inheritance is not limitation. Our inheritance is the knowledge that limitations are constructed, not natural — that they can be dismantled, one proof at a time, one experiment at a time, one discovery at a time.

The mind was never shackled. The shackles were always external. And the external can be removed.

The future is ours to invent.

CHAPTER FOUR

The Book Was Never Closed

A Tribute to Librarians and Keepers of Knowledge

Consider what it means to burn a library.

It means more than the destruction of paper and ink. It means the deliberate erasure of accumulated human thought — the ideas, discoveries, arguments, stories, and questions that a civilization has deemed worth preserving.

To burn a library is to say: this knowledge should not exist.

The people who produced it should be forgotten. Their contribution to the sum of human understanding should be unmade.

The library at Alexandria — the greatest repository of ancient knowledge the world had ever assembled — burned. The libraries of Timbuktu were looted and scattered and partially destroyed by Moroccan invaders in 1591. The books and documents of conquered and enslaved peoples throughout history have been among the first targets of the conqueror, because the conqueror understands something that the conquered sometimes forget: that a people who lose their records lose more than information. They lose their continuity. They lose the thread that connects them to their own past, and without that thread, they can be remade in the image the conqueror prefers.

This is why literacy was made criminal under American slavery. This is why, after emancipation, Black schools were burned and Black libraries were vandalized and Black newspapers were suppressed. This is why, in our own time, there are movements to remove books by and about Black people from school libraries and curricula. The target is always the same: the knowledge that allows a people to know themselves.

But here is what the burners of libraries have never fully understood: you cannot burn what has been memorized.

You cannot suppress what has been passed, mouth to ear, generation to generation. You cannot destroy a people's knowledge of themselves if that knowledge lives not only in books but in the bodies of the people — in the stories they tell their children at night, in the songs they sing at church, in the recipes they cook at holidays, in the names they give their babies, names that reach back across the Atlantic to languages and cultures that slavery tried and failed to sever.

The book was never closed. Because the book was never only made of paper.

The Griot Tradition and the First Libraries

Long before the first public library opened its doors in America, long before the printing press made books available to anyone who could afford them, the knowledge of African civilizations was preserved in a form more durable than paper: human memory, trained and disciplined to a purpose.

The griots of West Africa — the djeli in Mande languages, the gewel among the Wolof — were not merely storytellers.

They were the living archives of their societies. A master griot might carry in memory the complete genealogical history of a royal family going back thirty generations, the diplomatic history of relations between kingdoms, the oral texts of hundreds of songs and epic poems, the precedents by which disputes were to be resolved, the names of the dead and the manner of their dying.

This knowledge was transmitted through years of apprenticeship, beginning in childhood, requiring the development of memory techniques and performance skills that constituted a complete educational system. The griot's art was both science and art — the science of accurate retention and the art of living transmission, of making dead history feel present and immediate.

When the slave ships came, the griots who survived the Middle Passage carried their libraries in their minds.

Stripped of every material possession, they carried something that could not be confiscated. And in the enslaved communities of the Americas — in the hush harbors where enslaved people gathered secretly to pray, in the fields where they sang work songs whose coded content their enslavers did not understand, in the quarters where grandmothers told grandchildren the stories of where they came from — the griot tradition found new forms.

The sorrow songs. The spirituals. The blues. These were not merely music. They were archives. They carried history and theology and community and resistance in forms that the enslaver could not easily decode. "Steal Away to Jesus" was a signal for secret meetings. "Follow the Drinking Gourd" was a map to freedom, the drinking gourd being the Big Dipper, pointing north. The songs were libraries.

The singers were librarians.

The Crime of Reading

Under the slave codes of the American South, teaching an enslaved person to read or write was a criminal offense.

The penalties were severe. The reasoning was explicit and has been recorded: if the enslaved could read, they could access the abolitionist literature that was circulating. They could forge passes and travel documents. They could read the newspapers and know that there were people fighting for their freedom. They could, most dangerously of all, read the Declaration of Independence and the Constitution — documents that proclaimed the self-evident truth of human equality — and understand the full depth of the hypocrisy they were living under.

Knowledge, the slaveholder understood, was freedom. Or at least, it was the first step toward freedom. And so knowledge was made criminal.

But the hunger for knowledge cannot be legislated away.

Frederick Douglass, as he described in his autobiography, began his education when the wife of his enslaver, Sophia Auld, began teaching him the alphabet. Her husband stopped her — explaining the dangers of literacy to her in terms that Douglass, listening, found revelatory. "What he most dreaded," Douglass wrote, "that I most desired." He

then proceeded to educate himself by any means available —
trading bread with the white boys in the neighborhood for
reading lessons, studying every piece of printed material he
could get his hands on, learning to write by tracing the letters
in the spelling books of the Auld children.

He was not alone. Throughout the South, enslaved
people were teaching themselves and each other to read in
secret — in hidden rooms, under cover of darkness, at
personal risk of severe punishment. The hunger was
irrepressible.

The knowledge, once tasted, could not be untasted.

And when emancipation came, the first thing freed
people did — even before they had stable housing, even before
they had secured their economic survival — was build schools.
The Freedmen's Bureau reported that by 1870, more than
4,000 schools had been established for formerly enslaved
people. Many were in church buildings.

Many were in the homes of teachers who received no
pay.

Many were burned by white mobs who understood that educated Black people were a threat to the system of racial hierarchy that slavery had sustained.

They burned the schools. The freed people rebuilt them.

The Librarians of the Segregated South

In the cities and towns of the Jim Crow South, public libraries were for white patrons only. Black citizens — who paid the same taxes that funded those libraries — were refused entry, refused borrowing privileges, refused the basic civic resource of access to books.

And so, in city after city, Black communities built their own.

The Louisville Free Public Library for Colored Persons opened in 1905, funded by a combination of public money — finally and grudgingly acknowledged to be owed — and private donations from the Black community. The 135th Street Branch of the New York Public Library in Harlem, opened in

1905, became under the leadership of librarian Ernestine Rose and, crucially, through the donation of the collection of Arturo Alfonso Schomburg, a Puerto Rican of African descent, one of the great archives of Black history and culture in the world. The Schomburg Center for Research in Black Culture, as it is now known, holds more than 11 million items — manuscripts, photographs, recordings, films, artifacts — documenting the African diaspora.

Arturo Schomburg had been told by a teacher in Puerto Rico that Black people had no history, no heroes, no accomplishments worth recording. He spent the rest of his life proving that teacher wrong. He collected books and manuscripts and artwork and artifacts from throughout the African diaspora, amassing over the decades a collection of staggering scope and significance. In 1926 he sold it to the New York Public Library — not for profit but for preservation, for accessibility, for the future students and scholars who would need it. He then became the curator of the collection he had donated.

He gave his library away so that everyone could have it.

This is what keepers of knowledge do. They understand that the value of what they hold is realized not in possession but in sharing — that a library's purpose is not to accumulate but to transmit, not to preserve for its own sake but to keep alive what would otherwise die.

Carter G. Woodson and the Father of Black History

In 1915, Carter G. Woodson founded the Association for the Study of Negro Life and History. He was the son of formerly enslaved parents, had worked in the coal mines of West Virginia as a young man, had educated himself largely on his own before entering formal schooling at the age of twenty, and had earned a doctorate from Harvard — one of the first African Americans to do so.

He looked at what American education was teaching Black children about themselves, and he was appalled. The history they were being taught was a history from which they had been erased — or worse, in which they appeared only as property, as problem, as the passive objects of other people's decisions, never as agents of their own destiny, never as contributors to the civilization that had been built so substantially on their labor.

He understood what this did to a people. He had felt it himself. He had seen it in the children he taught. And he set out to correct it with the systematic thoroughness of a scholar who understood that the correction of a lie requires something more than assertion — it requires documentation, publication, and persistent repetition in the face of a culture that prefers the comfortable lie.

He founded what would become the Journal of Negro History, and later the Negro History Bulletin, and he published, year after year, the scholarship that was recovering and establishing the record of Black achievement and Black history that the mainstream academy was ignoring. He established Negro History Week in 1926 — choosing the second week of February because it contained the birthdays of both Frederick Douglass and Abraham Lincoln — as an annual occasion for schools and communities to engage with Black history.

It was extended to Black History Month in 1976, though Woodson himself had argued from the beginning that Black history should be integrated into education year- round, not sequestered in a week or a month as though it were a specialty item rather than an essential component of the full story of American life.

He wrote: "If you can control a man's thinking you do not have to worry about his action. When you determine what a man shall think, you do not have to concern yourself about what he will do. If you make a man feel that he is inferior, you do not have to compel him to accept an inferior status, for he will seek it himself."

He was describing a mechanism of oppression. He was also, implicitly, describing its antidote: teach a people their history accurately and completely, and they will not accept an inferior status, for they will know that no such status is warranted.

This is the work of the keeper of knowledge. Not neutral preservation, but active resistance. Not simply collecting what exists, but ensuring that what would otherwise be lost is found and held and made available to those who need it.

Mary McLeod Bethune and the Archive of a Life

Mary McLeod Bethune was born in 1875 in Mayesville, South Carolina, the fifteenth of seventeen children of formerly enslaved parents. She walked miles to school and understood from the beginning that her education was not a personal luxury but a communal responsibility — that what she learned, she would teach; that every door opened to her was meant to be held open for those behind her.

She founded a school in Daytona Beach, Florida, in 1904, with $1.50 in capital and a building she rented for eleven dollars a month. She sold pies and chicken and ice cream to raise money for supplies. She turned the school into a full institution — the Daytona Educational and Industrial Training

School for Negro Girls, which eventually became Bethune-Cookman University.

She became advisor to presidents. She was appointed by Franklin Roosevelt to his "Black Cabinet," serving as Director of Negro Affairs for the National Youth Administration, the highest federal position held by a Black American at that time. She was the only Black woman to participate in the founding conference of the United Nations in San Francisco in 1945.

And throughout all of this, she kept records. She saved letters. She preserved documents. She understood that the archives of her life and work were not personal property but historical necessity — that the story of what she had built and who she had fought and what she had achieved was a story that belonged to her people and to history.

When she died in 1955, she left behind not only her institutions but something she had written called "My Last Will and Testament" — not a legal document but a spiritual one, a message to the Black people of America and to all who would come after. It is not a long document, but it is a vast one. She left, she wrote, love and hope and the thirst for education, a belief in the dignity of the human person, a desire to harmonize and unite the races, and what she called "a responsibility to our young people."

"I leave you," she wrote, "a thirst for education.

Knowledge is the prime need of the hour."

She was right in 1955. She is right now.

The Libraries We Built

Throughout the twentieth century, Black communities across America built libraries, collected books, and established archives with the resources available to them — which were rarely sufficient and always hard-won.

The Schomburg was only the most famous example. In city after city, Black librarians — the majority of them women, because librarianship was one of the few professional fields open to Black women with advanced education — built and maintained collections that preserved what the mainstream would not. They ordered books from publishers who did not market to Black readers. They cataloged materials in systems that required them to create categories that the Library of Congress had not bothered to establish. They served communities that depended on them not just for books but for information about legal rights, about social services, about the practical knowledge that helps people navigate systems designed to exclude them.

These women — and they were mostly women — were the inheritors of the griot tradition in the most direct sense.

They were the keepers of the community's knowledge.

Their libraries were the community's memory.

What Is At Stake Now

We are living in a moment when the effort to close the book has intensified. Books by Black authors are among those most frequently challenged and removed from school libraries. Curricula that include the full history of American slavery and its consequences are being restricted by legislation. University diversity offices — the institutional expression of the commitment to include Black voices and perspectives in higher education — are being defunded and dismantled. The Tuskegee Airmen's portraits have been removed from military websites. The statues of Black heroes have been bypassed for removal while the statues of confederate traitors are defended as history.

This is the old pattern, wearing new clothes. The machinery of erasure, as functional as ever, applied now not with slave codes and night riders but with legislation and school board votes and executive orders.

And the response must be the same as it has always been.

We remember. We record. We teach.

We become, each of us, keepers of the knowledge that the world would prefer to lose. We tell our children the full story — not the comfortable version, not the version that ends with triumph and skips the cost, but the full story, with all its pain and all its glory. We support the libraries and the archives and the scholars and the teachers who do this work. We understand that to preserve memory is not a passive act. It is resistance. It is revolution.

It is, as Carter G. Woodson understood, the most fundamental act of freedom.

The book was never closed.

The ledger was never empty.

The memory was never lost.

And as long as we keep telling,

as long as we keep writing,

as long as we keep teaching —

it never will be.

CHAPTER FIVE

The Hand Was Never Empty

A Tribute to Black Artists and Builders

Art is the oldest human technology. Before the wheel, before agriculture, before the first city rose from the banks of the first great river, human beings were making images on stone walls, shaping figures from clay, decorating their tools and their bodies and their dead. They were saying, through these acts, something that no other technology has ever said as clearly: we are conscious. We notice. We find meaning in what we see. We need to express that meaning. We are, in the deepest sense, makers.

The oldest known examples of human art were found in Africa. The ochre engravings discovered at Blombos Cave in South Africa date to approximately 75,000 years ago.

The painted stones found at Wonderwerk Cave in the Northern Cape have been dated to more than 500,000 years ago. The tradition of art — of making meaning visible — is older than our species as we currently define it, and it is African.

From this root, a tradition grew that encompasses the pyramids and the Benin Bronzes, the rock churches of Ethiopia and the quilts of Gee's Bend, Alabama, the canvases of Jacob Lawrence and the installations of Kara Walker, the street art of Jean-Michel Basquiat and the sculptures of Elizabeth Catlett.

It is one tradition, continuous across millennia, interrupted but never severed by the forced diaspora of slavery. It is the tradition of people who have always understood that the hand is never empty — that to make is to affirm, and to affirm is to live, and to live, in the fullest sense, is to create.

The First Art of the World

In the Sahara, before it became a desert — when it was a green and fertile landscape supporting complex human societies — our ancestors painted the rocks with images of cattle and hunters and dancers and the animals that shared their world. These paintings, found in sites across the Saharan region from Morocco to Sudan, are thousands of years old, and they are beautiful. They are not crude or primitive. They represent animals with an accuracy and a grace that tells us their makers were careful observers and skilled craftspeople. They represent people in motion with an energy that is still, ten thousand years later, kinetic — you can feel the dance, the hunt, the festival.

This is the beginning. Not of African art alone. Of human art.

The Egyptian civilization that followed — which was, in its early centuries, a civilization of dark-skinned African people, whatever later dynasties may have introduced — produced art of such sustained excellence and such wide influence that it shaped the aesthetics of every civilization that came after it. The clean lines and hierarchical scale of Egyptian painting. The monumental sculpture of the pharaohs. The delicate gold work of the tomb goods, the jewelry, the decorated furniture. The murals of everyday life — bakers and brewers, farmers and fishermen, musicians and dancers — that cover the walls of tombs intended to make the afterlife feel familiar and welcoming.

These are not footnotes to the history of art. They are its foundation.

The Benin Kingdom and Its Bronzes

In the kingdom of Benin, in what is now southern Nigeria, beginning around the thirteenth century, a tradition of bronze casting developed that produced works of art that remain, seven hundred years later, among the most technically accomplished and aesthetically extraordinary objects ever made by human hands.

The Benin Bronzes — a term used to describe hundreds of brass plaques, sculptures, and objects created by the royal craftspeople of Benin — were made using the lost-wax casting technique, a process of extraordinary complexity and precision that produces surfaces of remarkable detail.

The plaques depict court ceremonies, battles, and the figures of kings and warriors and court officials with a

specificity that makes them simultaneously art and history —
documents of a civilization recording itself with care and pride.

When British soldiers looted the royal palace of Benin
in 1897 — an act of colonial violence that destroyed a
civilization's center of political and cultural life — they found,
among the treasures they carried off, these bronzes.

They were bewildered. They had not expected to find
evidence of sophisticated artistic achievement in what they had
been prepared to think of as a primitive society. Some of them
concluded that the bronzes must have been made by
Europeans, perhaps ancient Greeks or Portuguese traders. The
idea that Africans had made them was, to the colonial mind,
simply unacceptable.

The bronzes were distributed to museums throughout
Europe, where they remain to this day, in many cases, despite
decades of demands for their return. The British Museum
holds more than 900 of them. The Met in New York holds
more. Germany has been among the few countries to begin
returning some of its holdings.

They belong in Benin. They are Benin's story, told in metal with a mastery that the thieves who took them could not replicate.

Augusta Savage and the Courage of the Sculptor

In 1923, Augusta Savage, a young Black sculptor from Green Cove Springs, Florida, applied for a summer art program in France funded by the French government and the American committee overseeing an art competition.

She was rejected. The reason given, eventually and reluctantly, was her race. Two white women on the selection committee reportedly refused to travel to France on the same ship as a Black woman.

The rejection became public. There was outrage in some quarters. A New York newspaper ran a headline about the discrimination. Augusta Savage used the attention to make her case — not simply for herself but for the principle that artistic talent is not a racial characteristic, that the gates of art education should not be governed by the gates of Jim Crow.

She did not get to go to France that summer. She kept making art.

She made portraits — of W.E.B. Du Bois, of Marcus Garvey, of a young boy from her Harlem neighborhood that she called Gamin and that became one of the most reproduced sculptures of the Harlem Renaissance. She established the Savage Studio of Arts and Crafts in Harlem, offering free art instruction to hundreds of young people who could not afford commercial art classes. She was appointed director of the Harlem Community Art Center, funded by the Federal Art Project.

Her most famous work, The Harp, was commissioned for the 1939 World's Fair in New York. It depicted a choir of Black figures arranged in the shape of a harp, their mouths open in song, with a large hand below suggesting the hand of God that gives voice to music. It stood sixteen feet tall.

It was celebrated by everyone who saw it. When the World's Fair ended, it was destroyed — the logistics and expense of preserving it were not prioritized. Only photographs and a small plaster model remain.

She kept making art.

She kept teaching.

She left behind, in the students she trained and the community she built and the example she set, a legacy larger than any individual sculpture.

Jacob Lawrence and the Migration Series

In 1940 and 1941, a twenty-three-year-old Black artist named Jacob Lawrence completed a series of sixty paintings that told the story of the Great Migration — the movement of more than six million Black Americans from the South to the North between 1910 and 1970, one of the largest internal migrations in American history.

He worked in a style that was flat and bold and entirely his own — figures simplified to their essential shapes, colors strong and unmodulated, compositions designed to carry maximum emotional and narrative force with minimum visual fuss. He had learned from the Harlem Renaissance artists who surrounded him. He had learned from the Mexican muralists. He had learned from the cubists. And he had transformed all of it into something that belonged only to him and to the story he was telling.

The Migration Series was acquired jointly by the Museum of Modern Art and the Phillips Collection, the first major work by a Black artist to enter the collections of both institutions. It was reproduced in Fortune magazine,

bringing it to a national audience. It told the story of Black Americans leaving the terror of the South — the sharecropping and the lynchings and the Jim Crow laws — and arriving in the North, which offered different freedoms and different restrictions.

Lawrence went on to create other series: on Toussaint L'Ouverture, on Frederick Douglass, on Harriet Tubman, on John Brown. He taught for decades at the University of Washington. He painted with the conviction that art has a responsibility — not propaganda, not sloganeering, but the deeper responsibility of bearing witness accurately and with the full force of artistic vision to the truths that the world would prefer to look away from.

Elizabeth Catlett: Testimony in Bronze and Wood

Elizabeth Catlett was born in Washington, D.C., in 1915, the granddaughter of enslaved people. She studied art at Howard University, then applied to the graduate program at the Carnegie Institute of Technology, which rejected her because of her race. She enrolled instead in the program at the University of Iowa, studying under Grant Wood, and became the first student to earn a master of fine arts degree from that program.

Her thesis sculpture was a mother holding a child — a subject she would return to throughout her career, because in it she found the distilled essence of what she was trying to say: that Black life, in its most ordinary and intimate moments, contains a beauty and a dignity and a sacred quality that art has a responsibility to make visible.

She spent much of her adult life in Mexico, where the artistic culture was more welcoming to her work and to her politics than Cold War America, which placed her on the Un-American Activities Committee's list of subversives.

She married the Mexican muralist Francisco Mora and raised her family there. She became a Mexican citizen.

But she never stopped being an artist of and for Black people. Her sculpture Singing Head carries in its upturned face an expression of such complex emotion — suffering and determination and transcendence combined — that it reads as a portrait not of a single woman but of an entire people's experience. Her linocut prints of Black women workers, of Harriet Tubman, of Sojourner Truth, of sharecroppers and mothers and activists, are documents of Black female experience so precise and so compassionate that they constitute a kind of visual literature.

She received the National Medal of Arts in 2003. She lived to be ninety-six years old, making art nearly until the end.

She said: "Art should be for the liberation of the people."

She meant it.

She proved it.

The Street as Canvas: Jean-Michel Basquiat

In the late 1970s and early 1980s, a young man of Haitian and Puerto Rican descent named Jean-Michel Basquiat was writing on the walls of lower Manhattan under the name SAMO — "same old shit" — aphorisms and observations that combined the visual language of street art with the intellectual sophistication of a voracious, self- educated mind.

He was seventeen years old.

By the time he was twenty-one, his paintings were hanging in galleries. By twenty-two he had been featured on the cover of the New York Times Magazine. By twenty-three he was one of the most celebrated artists in the world.

His work defied easy categorization. He painted on canvas and on doors and on windows and on refrigerators. He incorporated words and diagrams and anatomy charts and references to jazz and boxing and African history and street life and colonialism and the experience of being young and Black and brilliant in a world that wanted to consume his talent without acknowledging his humanity.

He painted crowns — the crown was his signature, his proclamation that Black men are royalty, that the streets they walk are their kingdom, that the genius working through them is worthy of recognition.

He died in 1988, of a heroin overdose. He was twenty-seven years old.

His work sells today for tens of millions of dollars.

Museums compete for it. Collectors guard it. The world that consumed him in life without fully seeing him celebrates him in death with the enthusiasm of a culture that prefers its Black geniuses safely historical.

But the paintings are still speaking. They always will be.

Kara Walker and the Silhouette as Reckoning

Kara Walker works in silhouette — cut paper, black on white, the most reductive and the most devastating visual language possible. Her large-scale installations fill entire gallery walls with images drawn from the iconography of antebellum American history: plantation life, slavery, sexual violence, power, and humiliation, rendered in a graphic style that is simultaneously beautiful and horrifying.

She forces the viewer to look. She makes looking a moral act. You cannot stand before a Kara Walker installation and remain neutral. You cannot maintain the comfortable distance that American culture has traditionally offered white viewers when engaging with the history of slavery — the sense that it was long ago, that it is settled, that the proper response is mild regret followed by forward motion.

Her silhouettes will not allow it. They insist on the specificity of the violence. They insist on the personhood of the people subjected to it. They insist on the connection between that history and this present.

She received the MacArthur Genius Grant in 1997 at the age of twenty-eight. She is one of the most important artists of her generation, of any background. She says what needs to be said in the visual language that can say it most effectively.

The hand was never empty.

Look at what it has made.

Look at what it refuses to let us forget.

CHAPTER SIX

The Body Was Never Broken

A Tribute to Black Athletes

The body remembers what the mind sometimes forgets.

In the highlands of Ethiopia, where the altitude demands more of the lungs and the heart, young men and women rise before the sun and run. They run on red dirt roads through eucalyptus forests and over the ridges of hills that catch the first light of morning. They run as their parents ran and their grandparents ran — not only for competition, though the competition has produced some of the fastest long-distance runners the world has ever seen, but because running is part of who they are, part of how the body knows itself, part of the ancient covenant between the human animal and the earth it moves across.

The body remembers.

It remembers the savannas of East Africa, where our shared ancestors first stood upright and discovered what the bipedal form can do — that running on two legs, though slower than most quadrupeds over short distances, is uniquely suited for long distances, for the persistent hunt, for covering the ground between water and food and safety. The human body is, in its basic architecture, an endurance machine. And the people from whom all humanity descends — the people of Africa — have been perfecting the use of that machine for longer than any other people on earth.

This is not metaphor. This is evolutionary biology.

The body was never broken. It was built to soar.

Jesse Owens and the Defeat of a Philosophy

On August 3, 1936, Jesse Owens walked into Olympic Stadium in Berlin, Germany, with the eyes of the world upon him and the weight of a particular kind of history pressing down on the moment.

Adolf Hitler had conceived of the 1936 Berlin Olympics as a showcase for the Nazi theory of Aryan racial supremacy.

The German team was to demonstrate, on the field and on the track, the physical superiority of the Aryan race. The presence of Black athletes on the American team was, from the Nazi perspective, an embarrassment that the results would soon resolve.

Jesse Owens proceeded to win four gold medals.

He won the 100 meters, the 200 meters, the long jump, and the 4x100 relay. He set or equaled world records in each event. He was the most celebrated athlete of the Games. Seventy years later, he remains one of the most recognized names in the history of the Olympics.

The legend holds that Hitler refused to acknowledge Owens's victories, that he turned away or left the stadium.

The historical record is more complicated — Hitler had been instructed by the International Olympic Committee not to offer personal congratulations to any athlete — but the meaning of the moment was not complicated. A Black man from Cleveland, Ohio, the son of a sharecropper, had gone to the capital of the Third Reich and disproved its central premise in the most public, most dramatic, most irrefutable way possible.

He did not do it with words. He did it with his body. He did it with the 10.3 seconds it took him to run 100 meters, with the 8.06 meters he covered in a single long jump, with the physical fact of his excellence, undeniable and permanent in the record books.

He came home to a hero's welcome in New York — a ticker tape parade. Then he returned to Ohio and was unable to find work commensurate with his abilities. He raced against horses and motorcycles for money. The country that had sent him to disprove the Nazi theory of racial hierarchy did not feel obligated to extend to him the full benefits of the democracy he had represented.

He said, later in life, that Hitler had not snubbed him. He said that Franklin Roosevelt had not sent him a telegram of congratulations or invited him to the White House. His exact words: "Hitler didn't snub me — it was FDR who snubbed me. The president didn't even send me a telegram."

The body had performed its miracle. The country was not yet ready to receive the man.

Jackie Robinson and the Integration of Baseball

There is a reason that Jackie Robinson's number — 42 — is retired across all of Major League Baseball, the only number so honored league-wide. There is a reason that every April 15, on Jackie Robinson Day, every player in every game wears the number 42. There is a reason that when we speak of integration in American sports, the conversation always returns, ultimately, to Jackie Robinson.

It is not only because he was an extraordinary baseball player, though he was — a natural athlete who had starred in baseball, football, basketball, and track at UCLA, who could have been a professional in any of the four sports he played. It is because of what he agreed to do and how he did it.

Branch Rickey, the general manager of the Brooklyn Dodgers, had decided to break the color line in Major League Baseball. He had scouted Black players for years.

He chose Robinson not only for his athletic ability but for his character — specifically, Rickey told him, he needed a man strong enough not to fight back.

Robinson, who was by nature combative and who had already faced a court martial in the Army for refusing to move to the back of a military bus, understood the assignment. He agreed. He spent his first two years in professional baseball absorbing racist abuse — from opposing players, from crowds, from hotel desk clerks who refused him rooms and restaurant owners who refused him service — and responding not with the fury he felt but with performance. He responded on the field, where the rules were clear and the excellence was inarguable.

He won the first Rookie of the Year award in baseball history. He won the MVP award. He was a six-time All- Star. He helped lead the Brooklyn Dodgers to six National League pennants. He was inducted into the Hall of Fame in 1962, his first year of eligibility.

And after baseball, he did not retire quietly. He became a civil rights activist, speaking out against segregation with the same directness that had made him a target on the baseball field. He marched. He organized. He used the platform his athletic career had given him for something beyond athletics — for the full freedom that he understood the integration of baseball had only begun to address.

He said: "A life is not important except in the impact it has on other lives."

The impact of his life is immeasurable.

Muhammad Ali: The Greatest as Political Actor

Cassius Clay won the Olympic gold medal in boxing at the 1960 Rome Olympics, came home to Louisville, Kentucky, and was refused service at a restaurant. He reportedly threw his medal into the Ohio River. The story may be apocryphal. What is not apocryphal is the fury behind it — the recognition that no amount of athletic achievement would purchase the dignity that should have been his by birth.

He became Muhammad Ali. He became, arguably, the greatest boxer in history. He was fast in a way that heavyweight boxers were not supposed to be fast, precise in a way that brawlers were not supposed to be precise, intelligent about the sport in a way that fighters were not supposed to be intelligent. He moved around the ring with a dancer's economy of motion and struck with a physicist's understanding of force and angle and timing.

And he refused to go to Vietnam.

In 1967, when he was the heavyweight champion of the world at the height of his athletic powers, he refused induction into the United States Army. He said he had no quarrel with the Viet Cong. He said no Viet Cong had ever called him the word that white racists used. He said his conscience and his religion would not allow him to participate in a war he considered unjust.

He was stripped of his title. He was convicted of draft evasion. He was banned from boxing for three and a half years — three and a half years taken from the prime of a career that was already, objectively, one of the greatest in the history of sport.

He appealed. The Supreme Court, in 1971, overturned his conviction unanimously.

He returned to boxing and reclaimed his title — twice. He lit the Olympic flame at the 1996 Atlanta Games, his hand trembling from the Parkinson's disease that had taken his speed and his precision, but his face still carrying the beauty and the defiance that had always been its most essential quality.

He was not the greatest only in the ring. He was the greatest because he understood that the ring was not big enough to contain what he had to say.

The Williams Sisters and the Democratization of Excellence

The story of Venus and Serena Williams is, in some respects, the most improbable in the history of American sport.

They grew up in Compton, California, a neighborhood that is not associated with tennis — a sport that has historically been the province of the country club, the private court, the world of white wealth. Their father, Richard Williams, had written a plan for raising tennis champions before either of his daughters was born. He taught himself the game from instructional videos. He taught his daughters on public courts in Compton, a decision that required him to run off gang members and navigate the general indifference of a tennis establishment that did not see itself in the family from Compton.

Venus turned professional at fourteen. Serena at fifteen.

Both became champions — but not without resistance from a tennis world that received them with something between condescension and open hostility. There were players who made racist comments about them. There were spectators who booed them. There were tournament officials who seemed, at times, to be operating by different rules when the Williams sisters were involved.

They kept playing. They kept winning.

Between them, they have won more Grand Slam singles titles than any other pair of siblings in tennis history.

Serena has won twenty-three Grand Slam singles titles, the most by any player — man or woman — in the Open Era.

She is, by most measures, the greatest tennis player of all time.

She played through pregnancy complications that left her fighting for her life. She returned from near death to compete at the highest level of her sport. She used her platform to speak about the way the American medical system failed Black women, about the unconscious bias that led the medical staff caring for her after her daughter's birth to initially dismiss her concerns about her own condition — concerns that, if left unaddressed, could have killed her.

She was not merely an athlete. She was a witness. And her testimony extended far beyond the baseline.

The Body as Protest: Tommie Smith and John Carlos

On October 16, 1968, at the Summer Olympics in Mexico City, Tommie Smith and John Carlos stood on the medal podium after finishing first and third in the 200-meter sprint. They were American men. They had just performed at the highest level of their sport on the world's largest stage.

They bowed their heads as the national anthem played.

They raised their fists.

Smith wore a black glove on his right hand, Carlos on his left — they had each brought one glove, and when Carlos left his behind, they shared Smith's pair. Smith wore a black scarf around his neck, representing Black pride.

Carlos wore beads, representing the Black people who had been lynched or otherwise killed. Their feet were bare inside their shoes, representing Black poverty.

The gesture lasted perhaps thirty seconds. The image has lasted more than half a century.

They were expelled from the Olympic Village. They received death threats. Their athletic careers were effectively ended. The United States Olympic Committee condemned them. The sports establishment condemned them.

And history vindicated them.

The bronze statue of that moment stands today at San Jose State University, where both men had been students. In 2019, Sports Illustrated named it the most iconic sports image of the twentieth century. The raised fists, the bowed heads, the bare feet — they spoke a language that required no translation, about the gap between what America promised and what it delivered, about the right of Black athletes to be not only bodies in service of national pride but people with their own moral vision and their own right to express it.

The body was never only an instrument of sport. It was always also a statement.

It was always also a claim.

The body was never broken.

CHAPTER SEVEN

The Song Was Never Silent
A Tribute to Black Musicians and Carriers of Memory

In the beginning, there was rhythm.

Before melody, before harmony, before the concept of music as a separate category of human activity — before any of this, there was the human body keeping time. The heartbeat. The breath. The footfall. The clapping of hands around a fire that was both warmth and gathering, both light and language.

Rhythm is the oldest technology of human connection. It crosses every boundary that language erects — every barrier of dialect and vocabulary and reference. Two people who share no language can share a beat. Two people from opposite ends of the earth can feel the same rhythm in their bodies and, in that feeling, recognize each other as human.

This is why music was one of the primary things that enslaved Africans carried across the Atlantic. Not because they chose to carry music above other things — they were allowed to carry nothing. But rhythm, melody, the capacity for song, the understanding that music is both communication and communion — these lived in the body, and the body came.

And what was made from that — what emerged from the collision of African musical traditions with the languages and instruments and social contexts of the Americas — is one of the most extraordinary creative achievements in human history.

All of it. The spirituals and the blues and jazz and gospel and rhythm and blues and soul and funk and reggae and hip-hop — all of it flows from the same source: the music that survived the Middle Passage in the bodies of the enslaved.

This is not a metaphor. This is music history.

The Spirituals: Music as Survival and Resistance

The spirituals are the foundation. They are the oldest tradition of distinctly African American music, emerging from the enslaved communities of the American South in the eighteenth and early nineteenth centuries, and they are among the most profound examples of what human creativity can produce under conditions of extreme suffering.

They were, on one level, what they appeared to be: religious songs, expressions of Christian faith, requests for divine assistance in the face of earthly misery. "Go Down, Moses." "Swing Low, Sweet Chariot." "Deep River."

"Nobody Knows the Trouble I've Seen." They spoke of the

Old Testament's liberation narratives — of Moses leading his people out of Egypt — in terms that were transparently applicable to the situation of the enslaved and that were understood as such by both the singers and, increasingly, by the enslavers who tried to monitor and control them.

But they were also, beneath that surface, a fully developed code. "Swing Low, Sweet Chariot" was a reference to the Underground Railroad. "Follow the Drinking Gourd" gave navigational instructions for escape, the drinking gourd being the Big Dipper, which points to the North Star, which points north, toward freedom. "Wade in the Water" instructed freedom seekers to travel through water to throw off the dogs that might follow their scent.

They communicated when communication was forbidden.

They sustained community when community was being systematically destroyed. They preserved, in musical form, the traditions and the values and the communal identity that the institution of slavery was trying to eliminate.

Frederick Douglass understood this. He wrote of the spirituals with something close to reverence, describing them as the most eloquent expression of the sorrow and the hope and the endurance of his people. He understood that the power of the spirituals was not in their explicit content alone but in the act of their singing — in the communal affirmation that, however terrible the conditions, the people persisted, the spirit endured, the voice would not be silenced.

The spirituals are American music in the most fundamental sense: they were made here, from nothing but suffering and faith and the human need to make meaning from experience. And they are, at the same time, African music — in their rhythmic complexity, in their call- and-response structure, in the understanding they embody that music is not performance but participation, not spectacle but communion.

Mahalia Jackson: The Voice That Changed America

On August 28, 1963, more than 250,000 people gathered on the National Mall in Washington, D.C., for the March on Washington for Jobs and Freedom. Mahalia Jackson sang. She sang "How I Got Over" — a gospel song about perseverance, about the grace that sustains you through suffering — and the crowd moved with her, and the moment was one of those in which music and history and the longings of a people for justice came together in a convergence so powerful that those who were there described it in terms that reach for the supernatural.

Later, as Dr. King prepared to deliver the speech that would make history, as he seemed to be losing the thread of his prepared remarks, Mahalia Jackson, standing nearby, called to him: "Tell them about the dream, Martin."

He put down his notes.

He told them about the dream.

Whether the moment happened exactly as described, or whether it has been shaped by the retrospective light of legend, the spiritual truth of it is accurate: the gospel tradition — the music — was present at the creation of that speech. The speech and the song were from the same source. The preacher's cadence and the gospel singer's cadence are kin, and the kinship flows both ways — King's oratory was music, and Jackson's music was prophecy.

Mahalia Jackson had grown up in New Orleans, in a community so saturated with music that it was simply the medium through which life was lived. She moved to Chicago as a teenager, as part of the Great Migration, and began singing in church — in the small storefront churches of the Black

South Side, where gospel music was being transformed by Thomas Dorsey into something more rhythmically alive, more emotionally direct, more rooted in the blues than the traditional hymns had been.

She recorded. She toured. She became the most famous gospel singer in the world. She sang at presidential inaugurations. She refused to perform before segregated audiences.

She understood that her voice was not only hers. It was her people's voice, and she was its steward.

Louis Armstrong and the New Language

In 1923, in a recording studio in Richmond, Indiana, a young man from New Orleans named Louis Armstrong played a cornet solo on a record called "Chimes Blues." He was twenty-two years old. The music he played was different from anything anyone had recorded before — more complex, more personal, more inventive, more swinging. It was the sound of a musical language in the process of inventing itself.

Louis Armstrong did not invent jazz alone. Jazz was a communal creation, developed over decades in New Orleans and then Chicago and New York, by dozens of musicians of extraordinary ability who were building on African musical traditions, on the blues, on ragtime, on the church music they had grown up with. But Armstrong was its first great soloist — the first musician to demonstrate that within the collective tradition of jazz, there was room for an individual voice of such originality and power that it could change the way music was heard.

He played with a technical facility that was, simply, beyond what anyone had thought was possible on the trumpet. He played with a melodic imagination that produced solos of such beauty that musicians who heard them for the first time could not believe they were improvised — that a human being was inventing this, in real time, in the studio or on the bandstand, without a score. He sang with a voice that no one would have described as conventionally beautiful but that communicated, in every phrase, a warmth and a humor and a joy in existence that was irresistible.

He was not simply an entertainer, though he entertained brilliantly. He was a creator. He was making something new in the world. And what he made — the language of jazz improvisation, the language of swing, the language of the individual voice speaking within and against and in dialogue with the collective — that language spread throughout the world and changed music everywhere it went.

Billie Holiday and the Song That Ended a Practice

In 1939, Billie Holiday began performing a song called "Strange Fruit" — a song written by a white Jewish high school teacher from the Bronx named Abel Meeropol, who had written it as a poem after seeing a photograph of a lynching.

The song describes the bodies of lynched Black men hanging from poplar trees in the American South, using the language of horticulture — strange fruit, blood on the leaves, bodies in the southern breeze. It is one of the most devastating indictments of American racial violence ever committed to music. It is also one of the most beautiful songs ever recorded — the melody haunting, the arrangement spare, Holiday's voice navigating the words with such precision and such control that the emotional impact is, if anything, increased by the restraint.

Holiday's record label, Columbia, refused to record it. She recorded it for a small independent label. It became her signature song and one of the most celebrated recordings in American history. Time magazine called it the song of the century.

She performed it with a ritual she maintained throughout her career: the room would be darkened, all other lights extinguished, a single spot on her face. She would sing it, and then the lights would come up, and she would not speak, and she would leave the stage. She understood that some moments require not entertainment but witness — that to follow that song with another song would be a desecration.

Lynching did not end because of Billie Holiday. But the practice existed in a world in which "Strange Fruit" was being sung, and the world in which it was being sung was a world increasingly unable to sustain the comfortable lies that made lynching possible.

The song was never only a song. It was testimony. It was accusation. It was a demand.

Hip-Hop and the Contemporary Griot

In the late 1970s, in the South Bronx — a neighborhood that had been abandoned by the city, its buildings burned or deteriorating, its young people with nowhere to go and nothing to do — something happened at block parties.

DJs began isolating the percussion breaks in funk and soul records — the moments when everything dropped out except the drums — and looping them, extending them, creating a continuous rhythmic foundation over which young men began to speak. Not sing. Speak. Rap.

Improvise rhymes that described the world they were

living in, the people they knew, the injustices they saw and felt, the celebrations they wanted to stage.

It was, from the beginning, a griot tradition. Not metaphorically. Actually. The call-and-response. The community gathering. The commitment to documentation, to testimony, to speaking the truth about what was happening in a world that mainstream culture was not acknowledging.

Grandmaster Flash and the Furious Five released "The Message" in 1982, describing life in the South Bronx with a specificity and a darkness that popular music had not previously attempted: the broken glass, the pissy stairs, the welfare line, the prison sentence at the end of a life with no visible alternative. It was not entertainment. It was reportage. It was social documentation in rhyme.

Public Enemy made records that were alarms — that intended, explicitly, to wake people up, to make them angry, to make them informed about the history and the present of Black oppression in America. Chuck D called hip-hop the CNN of the Black community, and he was right: it reported what was happening in Black neighborhoods in a time when mainstream media was not reporting it.

Tupac Shakur wrote psalms of rage and tenderness and contradiction, describing the world as it was without pretending it was what it should be, and was killed at twenty-five with the songs still unwritten in him — a loss to American music as significant as any this country has sustained.

Lauryn Hill braided gospel and hip-hop and poetry into something that sounded like prophecy and moved the body and the spirit simultaneously. Her album The Miseducation of Lauryn Hill is one of the great American albums of any genre, in any period.

And Kendrick Lamar — from Compton, California, the city where Venus and Serena Williams learned to play tennis, the city where dreams are grown in soil that the country treats as disposable — Kendrick Lamar won the Pulitzer Prize for Music in 2018 for his album DAMN. He was the first non-classical, non-jazz musician to receive the award.

He received it because his music was doing what the Pulitzer Prize is supposed to recognize: making art of the highest order from the materials of American life, telling the truth about where we are and who we are, refusing comfort and demanding engagement.

He is the contemporary griot. He is Langston Hughes with a beat. He is Mahalia Jackson with a microphone. He is the latest expression of the oldest tradition.

The song was never silent.

Not in the ships.

Not in the fields.

Not in the church basements of the civil rights movement.

Not in the South Bronx block parties.

Not now.

The song continues, and it carries us, and it always will

CHAPTER EIGHT

The Classroom Was Never Empty

A Tribute to Black Educators

Education is not a gift that the powerful give to the powerless. It is a right that the powerful have always understood must be denied if the powerless are to remain so.

This is why the slave codes made literacy a crime. This is why, after the Civil War, schools for freed-eople were burned by white mobs with such regularity that the Freedmen's Bureau kept a running count. This is why, in the years of Jim Crow, Black schools received a fraction of the funding that white schools received. This is why, in our own time, schools in predominantly Black neighborhoods remain chronically underfunded, their buildings deteriorating, their teachers underpaid, their libraries inadequate.

It has always been understood, by those who benefit from Black oppression, that an educated Black person is a threat. Not a physical threat — though the paranoid logic of white supremacy has sometimes framed it that way — but a threat to the system of beliefs and arrangements that depends on Black people accepting their assigned place.

An educated person knows their rights. An educated person understands history. An educated person can speak and write and argue with precision. An educated person is equipped to demand what is owed and to recognize what has been taken.

This is why education has always been political.

And this is why Black educators — the men and women who have devoted their lives to teaching Black children the full truth of who they are and what they are capable of — have always been doing something more than teaching.

They have been doing something that their society, in many of its official expressions, has actively opposed.

They have been doing it anyway.

The first and most fundamental lesson of Black educational history is this: when the system will not educate you, you educate yourself.

Frederick Douglass's account of learning to read is one of the most remarkable passages in American autobiography.

He was an enslaved child in Baltimore, and his enslaver's wife had begun teaching him the alphabet before her husband put a stop to it, explaining that literacy would make an enslaved person unfit to serve. Douglass heard this and understood it — not as reason to abandon the pursuit but as the most compelling possible reason to pursue it. If literacy made a man unfit to be a slave, then literacy was what he needed.

He bribed the white boys of the neighborhood with bread — "my bread to them, their knowledge to me." He studied the spelling books he found in the house. He traced letters in the wood shavings at the shipyard where he was later sent to work. He taught himself to write by copying the letters carved into the timber.

By the time he escaped north, he was a fully literate man.

He used that literacy to write his autobiography, to edit newspapers, to deliver speeches that moved listeners to tears and to action, to correspond with presidents and abolitionists and world leaders. He became, through the exercise of the mind he had educated himself, one of the most consequential Americans of the nineteenth century.

His example became a model. Throughout Black American history, the self-educated man and woman — the person who sought knowledge despite the system that denied it — has been a recurring and essential figure. Not because formal education was not desired, but because when formal education was denied, the hunger for knowledge found another way.

Mary McLeod Bethune: Building the Future with $1.50

The story of Mary McLeod Bethune and the school she founded in Daytona Beach, Florida, in 1904 is, in every sense that matters, the story of Black education in America.

She arrived in Daytona Beach with a vision and $1.50. The vision was specific: a school for Black girls in a community that had no school for Black girls and no expectation of having one. The $1.50 was her entire capital.

She found a building. She rented it for eleven dollars a month. She could not afford eleven dollars a month, but she found ways — selling pies and chicken and sweet potato pudding to workers at a nearby construction site, knocking on doors in the white community and making her case for the importance of educating Black children, gathering small donations from Black community members who had little but understood what was at stake.

She made charcoal from burned logs for pencils. She used elderberries for ink. She made her students' desks from wooden crates. When she needed money for supplies, she found ways to get it. When she needed donations from wealthy white philanthropists, she found ways to make the case without compromising her dignity or her vision.

The school grew. It merged with a nearby boys' school and became Bethune-Cookman College. She served as president of it for decades. She served simultaneously as founder and leader of the National Council of Negro Women, which she established in 1935 to unify Black women's organizations across the country. She served as advisor to Franklin Roosevelt and later to Truman. She was, during the New Deal years, the highest-ranking Black person in the federal government.

And through all of it, she remained what she had always been: an educator. A woman who understood that the liberation of a people begins with their education, and that the education of a people begins with a single teacher willing to start with what she has.

She had $1.50.

She built a university.

The HBCU Tradition: Cathedrals of Learning

In the years following the Civil War, as freed-people across the South were building schools with their own hands and their own resources, a parallel effort was underway on a larger scale: the establishment of the institutions that would become Historically Black Colleges and Universities.

Howard University, founded in Washington, D.C., in 1867, was named for General Oliver Otis Howard of the Freedmen's Bureau. It was established as a comprehensive university — law, medicine, theology, education — intended to train the professionals and leaders that the newly freed Black community would need. It became, over the following century and a half, one of the most significant institutions of higher education in American history. Its law school, under Thurgood Marshall and others, developed the legal strategies that would eventually lead to Brown v. Board of Education. Its medical school trained Black doctors when white medical schools would not accept them. Its faculty and alumni have shaped every field of American intellectual and professional life.

Spelman College, founded in Atlanta in 1881 in the basement of a church with eleven students and two teachers, became the first historically Black college for women. Its graduates include Marian Wright Edelman, the children's rights advocate; Eslanda Robeson, the anthropologist; Alice Walker, the novelist and poet; and hundreds of thousands of other women who went on to build lives of meaning and achievement in every profession and every community.

Morehouse College, the men's liberal arts college in Atlanta, produced Martin Luther King Jr. and Spike Lee and Samuel L. Jackson and Maynard Jackson, the first Black mayor of Atlanta, and Howard Thurman, the theologian who was a mentor to King and a towering figure in American religious thought.

Tuskegee University gave us Booker T. Washington and the Tuskegee Airmen and generations of engineers and scientists and educators. Fisk University gave us W.E.B.

Du Bois and the Jubilee Singers. Hampton University gave us Booker T. Washington's education, which he then used to build Tuskegee.

These institutions exist because white America refused to educate Black Americans at equal institutions. They were built not as second choices but as acts of communal determination — the insistence that Black people would have institutions of higher learning worthy of the talent and the ambition that the community possessed in such abundance.

They are among the most important institutions in American history. They are the reason that, by any measure of professional achievement and intellectual contribution, Black America has produced so vastly more than anyone could have predicted given the obstacles placed before it.

Because the obstacles were met with institutions.

Because the exclusion was met with inclusion.

Because the burning of schools was met with the building of universities.

Thurgood Marshall and the Courtroom as Classroom

In 1954, Thurgood Marshall stood before the Supreme Court of the United States and made an argument that changed American history.

He was arguing Brown v. Board of Education — the consolidation of several cases challenging the "separate but equal" doctrine of Plessy v. Ferguson, the 1896 decision that had provided the constitutional framework for segregated schools throughout the South. Marshall, the chief legal counsel of the NAACP, had been building toward this moment for decades, winning case after case that chipped away at the foundations of legal segregation.

His argument drew on the work of psychologist Kenneth Clark, who had conducted experiments with Black children using black and white dolls — experiments that demonstrated that Black children, by the age of four, had already internalized the society's message that Black was inferior and white was superior. Segregation, Marshall argued, did not merely provide unequal resources. It did something more fundamental: it taught Black children that they were less. It embedded in their developing self- image the lie that American society most needed them to believe.

The Supreme Court agreed, unanimously, that separate educational facilities were inherently unequal.

The decision did not end segregation in American schools — that struggle continued for decades and continues today, in different forms. But it was a turning point. It was the moment when the legal framework that had sustained Jim Crow was cracked at its foundation.

Thurgood Marshall used education to fight for education.

He used the law — the most powerful instrument of the state — to argue that Black children deserved the same access to knowledge that white children were guaranteed.

He understood that the classroom was not merely a room with desks. It was the place where the next generation learned who they were and what they were capable of.

He made sure that what they would be taught, if he could help it, was the truth.

The Nobel Laureates: Black Scholars on the World Stage

The Nobel Prize is imperfect — its history reflects the biases of the culture that created it. But it remains the world's most recognized marker of intellectual achievement. And the Black scholars who have received it represent a tradition of intellectual excellence that stretches back to the first scholars of Timbuktu and the mathematicians of ancient Egypt.

Ralph Bunche received the Nobel Peace Prize in 1950 for his mediation of the 1948 Arab-Israeli armistice agreements — the first Black person to receive the award.

He had grown up in Los Angeles, graduated from UCLA, earned a doctorate from Harvard, and served as a senior official at the United Nations. He was a scholar and a diplomat and a civil rights activist, and he moved between these roles as though they were not separate callings but expressions of a single commitment to human dignity.

Martin Luther King Jr. received the Nobel Peace Prize in 1964, at thirty-five — the youngest person to receive the award at that time. He was in the middle of the most intense years of the civil rights movement, facing daily violence, constant surveillance by the FBI, and the hostility of a federal government that regarded him as a threat. He accepted the prize not as a personal honor but as recognition of the movement — of the thousands of ordinary people who had marched and sat in and been beaten and imprisoned in the service of a principle that should not have required a movement to establish.

Toni Morrison's Nobel lecture is itself a masterpiece of American prose. Wole Soyinka's Nobel lecture, delivered in 1986, was a meditation on African literature and its relationship to the colonial legacy that had attempted to suppress it. These were not acceptance speeches. They were intellectual performances of the highest order, delivered on the world's largest stage, saying: this tradition is real, this achievement is undeniable, and this recognition, however long delayed, is warranted.

The Teachers We Do Not Name

And then there are the teachers whose names are not in any record of distinguished alumni, whose work was never recognized by a Nobel committee or a literary prize or a presidential appointment.

The teacher in a one-room schoolhouse in the post-Reconstruction South who taught sixty students of varying ages with almost no supplies, who walked miles to her school because she could not afford a mule, who was paid a fraction of what her white counterpart earned, and who came back every day because she had looked into the eyes of her students and seen what was there, and understood that her job was to help them see it too.

The teacher in a segregated elementary school in Mississippi who covered the walls of her classroom with pictures of Black scientists and inventors and artists and leaders — not because she was required to, not because anyone was watching, but because she understood that children learn what they see, and she wanted her children to see themselves reflected in the record of human achievement.

The college professor at an HBCU who stayed when she could have gone to a more prestigious, better-funded institution, because she understood that her students needed her specifically — needed someone who looked like them and understood their experience and could tell them, with the authority of her own life, that the barriers were real and surmountable.

The teacher who bought school supplies with her own money. The teacher who stayed late. The teacher who made home visits. The teacher who remembered, ten years after a student graduated, what that student had been struggling with and asked about it when she saw her at the grocery store.

These teachers are not in this book by name because their names are too numerous. They are in this book by everything else — by the tradition they represent, by the work they did, by the students who carry their lessons in their bodies decades after the classroom has been left behind.

To learn was to resist.

To teach was to liberate.

We are heirs of both.

CHAPTER NINE

The Dream Was Never Deferred

A Tribute to Black Visionaries

In 1951, Langston Hughes published a poem that asked a question so simple and so devastating that it has never stopped being answered.

The poem was called "Harlem." It asked: what happens to a dream deferred?

It offered several possible answers. Does it dry up like a raisin in the sun? Fester like a sore? Crust and sugar over?

Does it sag like a heavy load? Or, the poem's final possibility, offered as a question with an explosive and ambiguous weight: does it explode?

Hughes was writing about Harlem, about the promises of the Great Migration that had not been kept, about the dreams that Black Americans had carried north and found still subject to the same gravity of racism in new clothes.

But he was also writing about something universal — about what happens to human aspiration when it is systematically denied. About the cost, paid by individuals and by societies, of refusing to let a people fully be what they are capable of being.

The answer, the century since has demonstrated, is: all of the above. Dreams deferred dry up and fester and sag and explode. They produce the despair and the fury and the creativity and the determination that have characterized Black American life in the century since Hughes wrote those lines. They produce the visionaries — the men and women who look at what is and refuse to accept that it is all that can be — who have driven not only Black progress but American progress, and who have demanded that the dream be made real.

Isabella Baumfree was born into slavery in New York State around 1797. She escaped in 1826, walked away from her enslaver carrying her infant daughter, and was sheltered by a Quaker family who helped her obtain her legal freedom. She changed her name, as many formerly enslaved people did, to mark the transformation: she became Sojourner Truth.

She was called by God, she said, to travel and preach. She traveled. She preached. She became one of the most powerful voices of both the abolitionist and early women's rights movements, speaking at conventions and churches and gatherings wherever she was welcomed and sometimes at gatherings where she was not.

In 1851, at the Women's Rights Convention in Akron, Ohio, she delivered a speech — or a series of remarks, or an improvised address, the exact form is disputed — that has become known as "Ain't I a Woman?" In it, she argued, from the evidence of her own life, that the femininity invoked to deny women's rights was a category that had never applied to her. She had plowed and planted and worked as hard as any man. No one had helped her into carriages or given her the best place in any room. She had borne children and watched them sold into slavery. If the category of "woman" was being used to limit women's rights, then the actual lives of Black women — who had been denied the protections that the category was supposed to extend — exposed the category as a myth.

She was not making an abstract argument. She was being the argument. Her body, her voice, her presence in that room was the refutation of every comfortable assumption that her audience had brought with them.

This is what Black visionaries have always done. They have used their lives as evidence. They have said: look at what is possible. Look at what we have built and written and discovered and created and endured. Look at what we are.

And then tell us again that your vision of us is accurate.

Ida B. Wells: The Journalist as Warrior

Ida Bell Wells was born in Holly Springs, Mississippi, in 1862, six months before the Emancipation Proclamation.

Her parents were enslaved. By the time she was sixteen, both of her parents had died of yellow fever and she was raising her five younger siblings.

She became a teacher. She became a journalist. She wrote for Black newspapers under the pen name Iola, with a directness and an incisiveness that quickly established her as one of the most important journalists of her era.

And then, in 1892, three of her friends — successful Black businessmen in Memphis — were lynched by a white mob.

The stated pretext was business competition: they had opened a grocery store that was taking customers from a white-owned store. The actual reason was the same as it always was: Black success, Black autonomy, Black refusal to accept white supremacy, was perceived as a threat that justified any violence.

Wells investigated. She published what she found. She found that the vast majority of lynchings were not, as the standard justification claimed, responses to attacks on white women. They were responses to Black economic success, to Black political organizing, to Black self-defense, to any expression of Black agency that the white power structure found threatening. The rape narrative was a cover story. The reality was terror in the service of control.

Her newspaper in Memphis was destroyed by a mob. She was warned that if she returned to Memphis she would be killed. She moved to Chicago. She continued writing and organizing and speaking. She toured England and Scotland, giving lectures that brought international attention to the practice of lynching in the American South at a time when the American government was not interested in addressing it.

She helped found the NAACP. She founded the Alpha Suffrage Club, one of the first Black women's suffrage organizations. She ran for the Illinois state legislature. She lived until 1931, fighting every day of her adult life for the proposition that Black lives matter — that the killing of Black people without legal consequence was not an unfortunate regional custom but a national emergency.

She was right. She spent her life being right. She was not adequately honored in her lifetime. She received the Pulitzer Prize posthumously in 2020 — 129 years after the journalism for which she received it.

The dream she carried never left her.

It was deferred.

It was not destroyed.

W.E.B. Du Bois: The Intellectual as Prophet

William Edward Burghardt Du Bois was born in Great Barrington, Massachusetts, in 1868, three years after the end of the Civil War. He grew up in a predominantly white community, was a brilliant student, was encouraged by his teachers, and won a scholarship to Fisk University in Nashville — his first sustained encounter with the Black South, which shocked and shaped him.

He earned a doctorate from Harvard in 1895 — the first Black person to do so — and went on to become a sociologist, historian, novelist, poet, editor, activist, and one of the most consequential thinkers of the twentieth century. His book The Souls of Black Folk, published in 1903, introduced the concept of the "double consciousness" — the "sense of always looking at oneself through the eyes of others, of measuring one's soul by the tape of a world that looks on in amused contempt and pity." This concept, derived from his own experience and expressed with the precision and the beauty of a first-rate literary intelligence, gave Black Americans a language for describing something they had always known but had not previously had such a precise formulation for: the psychological burden of living in a society that sees you as a problem rather than a person.

He co-founded the NAACP in 1909. He edited its magazine, The Crisis, for twenty-four years, turning it into one of the most important publications in American history. He wrote and wrote and wrote — history, sociology, poetry, fiction, autobiography, political philosophy — a body of work that rivals any American intellectual's in its scope and its significance.

He lived to be ninety-five years old. He died the day before the March on Washington — the day before Martin Luther King Jr. delivered the speech that drew on the same tradition of Black prophetic oratory that Du Bois had helped to shape. He had spent the last years of his life in Ghana, having renounced his American citizenship in frustration at the country's failure to live up to its promises.

He was right to be frustrated. He was right about almost everything. And the tradition of Black intellectual life in America is unimaginable without him.

Martin Luther King Jr.: The Dream Made Audible

On August 28, 1963, Martin Luther King Jr. stood at the Lincoln Memorial and delivered a speech that became the most quoted, most celebrated, most imitated speech in American history.

The speech is usually reduced to its most famous passage — the "I have a dream" section that begins two-thirds of the way through. The dream of a nation that lives up to its founding ideals. The dream of children judged not by the color of their skin but by the content of their character.

The dream of the sons of former slaves and the sons of former slaveholders sitting together at the table of brotherhood.

These are beautiful words. They are also, carefully read, radical ones. The table of brotherhood is a table of equality —

not charity, not tolerance, not the white majority's gracious inclusion of Black people in the national story, but actual equality, actual brotherhood, actual common stake in the common project.

And the parts of the speech that are less often quoted are more radical still. King described the "promissory note" of the Declaration of Independence and the Constitution — the promise that all men are created equal and endowed with unalienable rights — and declared that America had defaulted on this note when it came to its Black citizens.

He demanded that the note be honored. Not eventually.

Now. Not partially. Fully.

This is not the comfortable King of the inspirational poster. This is the King who, as the FBI wiretaps would confirm, was considered by J. Edgar Hoover to be the most dangerous man in America. The King who, in his later years, opposed the Vietnam War and spoke explicitly about the connection between racism and militarism and economic exploitation as three heads of the same beast.

The King who was organizing a Poor People's Campaign — a multiracial coalition demanding economic justice — when he was shot in Memphis, Tennessee, in April 1968.

He was thirty-nine years old.

The dream he articulated was not his alone. It was the dream of a people — the dream of everyone in the tradition from Phillis Wheatley to Frederick Douglass to Ida B.

Wells to W.E.B. Du Bois who had looked at America and said: you could be better than this. You should be better than this. We need you to be better than this.

The dream was never deferred in the sense of being abandoned.

It was deferred in the sense of being resisted.

And the resistance, however powerful, has never been powerful enough.

The dream persists.

Amanda Gorman: The Dream Renewed

On January 20, 2021, the day of Joseph Biden's inauguration as the 46th President of the United States, a twenty-two-year-old poet named Amanda Gorman stepped to the microphone on the steps of the Capitol.

Two weeks earlier, a mob had stormed that building in an attempt to overturn the results of a democratic election.

The wound was still raw. The symbolism of what was happening — a young Black woman reading her own words at the inauguration of the democracy that had failed her ancestors — was almost too much to hold.

She read "The Hill We Climb." She had written it in the days and weeks before the inauguration, and she had rewritten significant portions of it after January 6, incorporating the violence and the threat and the fragile persistence of democratic hope into a poem that refused to look away from the difficulty and refused to surrender the possibility.

"We will not march back to what was," she read, "but move to what shall be — a country that is bruised but whole, benevolent but bold, fierce and free."

She was not the end of a tradition. She was its latest expression — the newest voice in a conversation that has been going on since Phillis Wheatley wrote her first poem in colonial Boston, since the griots sang the histories of kings in the courts of Mali, since the first human being felt the need to say something that mattered and found a way to say it.

The dream was never deferred.

Not really.

It was being carried.

And it has been passed, hand to hand,

generation to generation,

from the first dawn to this morning.

CHAPTER TEN

The Gift Was Never Withheld

A Tribute to Black Philanthropists and Givers

The word "philanthropy" comes from the Greek: philos, loving, and anthropos, human being. Love of humanity.

The willingness to give — of time, of resources, of self — in service of the common good.

There is a story that American culture tells about philanthropy that begins with the Gilded Age, with the Rockefellers and the Carnegies and the Mellons, with the vast fortunes accumulated in the industrial economy and then, in part, redistributed through foundations and institutions that bear the philanthropists' names to this day. This is a real story. But it is not the whole story. And the part it omits is the part that tells us something more fundamental about what philanthropy actually is.

Because the deepest tradition of American philanthropy is not found in the foundation boardrooms. It is found in the collection plates of Black churches in the antebellum South, passed hand to hand in secret, gathering pennies from people who had nothing, to buy the freedom of those who had even less. It is found in the mutual aid societies that freed-people established the moment they were free — not waiting for permission or infrastructure, but building,

immediately and collectively, the institutions that their community would need to survive.

It is found in the grandmother who has never written a check to a foundation in her life, who has fed every hungry child who came to her door, who has paid the light bill for the family across the street when the lights were going to be cut off, who has given and given and given from a store that was never large enough and never ran out.

This is the tradition of Black philanthropy. It is older than the word.

The Mutual Aid Tradition

The institution of mutual aid — the practice of community members pooling resources to support each other in times of need — has roots in African social organization that predate the American experience. The communal ethic of many African societies — the understanding that the individual's well-being is inseparable from the community's well-being, that to have when others do not have is to have incompletely — was carried across the Atlantic and took new forms in the circumstances of the diaspora.

Under slavery, mutual aid was an act of profound resistance. When enslaved people shared food, when they cared for each other's children, when they organized to purchase the freedom of a community member, they were refusing the isolation that the system tried to enforce. They were insisting, against the institution's every effort to the contrary, that they were a community — that they had obligations to each other that transcended the relationships the system was designed to create.

After emancipation, mutual aid became structural. Black communities across the country established fraternal organizations, church-based benevolent societies, burial associations, credit unions, and insurance companies — institutions designed to provide, collectively, the security and opportunity that the broader society refused to extend individually. The African Methodist Episcopal Church's mutual aid programs. The Prince Hall Masons. The United Order of True Reformers. The Black-owned insurance companies that provided life insurance to Black policyholders when white insurance companies refused to cover them.

These institutions were philanthropy in its purest form: the love of humanity expressed through the practical work of ensuring that the vulnerable were protected, the bereaved were comforted, the ambitious were supported, and the community endured.

Madam C.J. Walker: The First Black Woman Millionaire

Sarah Breedlove was born in 1867 in Delta, Louisiana, the first member of her family born free. Her parents had been enslaved. She was orphaned at seven, married at fourteen to escape the household of a brutal brother-in-law, widowed at twenty with a two-year-old daughter, doing laundry for a living, watching her hair fall out from a scalp condition that was common among women who had limited access to clean water and proper nutrition.

She began experimenting with hair care products. She developed a formula and a method. She began selling it door to door, training other women to sell it as well, building, from nothing and from necessity, a network of sales agents that would eventually number 40,000 — all of them Black women, many of them previously employed as domestic workers, now earning independent incomes as entrepreneurs.

She became Madam C.J. Walker. She became the first Black woman millionaire in American history. She built a factory. She built a philanthropic organization. She gave to the NAACP's anti-lynching campaign. She gave to the YMCA. She gave to the scholarship fund that would educate the next generation of Black professionals.

She died in 1919 at fifty-one, from kidney failure complicated by high blood pressure — a condition that, like so many conditions that disproportionately affect Black Americans, was under-treated by a medical system that did not invest adequately in Black health.

She left most of her estate to educational and charitable causes.

She had arrived with nothing.

She had given everything.

Robert F. Smith and the Debt Forgiven

On May 19, 2019, Robert F. Smith stood at the podium at Morehouse College's commencement ceremony and said something that the graduating class of 2019 had not expected to hear.

He announced that he would pay off the student loan debt of the entire class.

It was approximately $34 million. He wrote the check.

Smith was a private equity billionaire — the richest Black man in America at the time, the founder of Vista Equity Partners, a software investment firm. He had grown up in a working-class family in Denver, had earned degrees from Cornell and Columbia, had built his fortune through two decades of financial work. He was not a public figure who had made his name through philanthropy. He was a businessman who had decided, at this particular moment, to do this particular thing.

The effect was not merely financial, though it was significantly financial. Student debt has a documented effect on the economic and personal choices of young people — the decision to take lower-paying jobs that serve communities, to start businesses, to have children, to buy homes. Eliminating the debt of 396 young Black men with one stroke of a pen was not a symbolic gesture. It was a material change in the possibilities available to those men and, by extension, to the families and communities they would go on to serve.

But it was also a symbol. It was a demonstration — visible, public, and dramatic — that Black wealth, when it exists, can be used in service of Black community. That the accumulation of resources is not an end in itself but a means, and that the end it most properly serves is the liberation and elevation of the people who, collectively, have always been denied the resources necessary for their own flourishing.

He said: "We're going to put a little fuel in your bus."

He put $34 million in the bus.

The bus is still running.

Oprah Winfrey: The Visible Gift

Oprah Winfrey was born in rural poverty in Kosciusko, Mississippi, in 1954. She was raised by her grandmother, then her mother, then her father. She was sexually abused as a child. She became a teenaged mother; her son died in infancy. She was told, repeatedly and by people in positions of authority over her career, that she was not suited for television.

She built a media empire. She became the first Black female billionaire in history. She did this in a country where every statistical measure of opportunity was stacked against her, in an industry that had no precedent for what she would become, through a combination of talent and intelligence and emotional honesty and the ability to make connection—genuine, human connection — across every barrier of race and class and geography that divides American life.

And she gave. She gave substantially and continuously and specifically. She established the Oprah Winfrey Leadership Academy for Girls in South Africa — a school for disadvantaged girls that has produced graduates who have gone on to universities worldwide. She established scholarships at Morehouse College and other HBCUs. She gave to disaster relief, to education, to healthcare. She gave to initiatives that addressed the specific vulnerabilities of Black women and girls. She gave, and gave, and gave.

And she used her platform — the most powerful media platform that any Black person in American history had ever held — to give something that does not appear on any accounting of charitable giving: visibility. She made Black stories visible to audiences that had never seen them. She championed books by Black authors. She gave voice to Black experiences that mainstream media had ignored or distorted. She understood that representation is a form of philanthropy — that to make a people visible is to give them something that money cannot purchase but that poverty of visibility can take away.

The Gift That Keeps Giving: Everyday Philanthropy

But the fullest expression of the tradition is not found in any endowment or foundation. It is found in the everyday acts of giving that have sustained Black communities through the centuries when no foundation existed and no endowment was possible.

The church. The Black church in America is not merely a religious institution. It is the oldest and most enduring philanthropic organization in the Black community. From the invisible church of enslaved people — gathering in secret, building community and solidarity and resistance in the only space available — to the great urban churches of the twentieth century, the Black church has been the place where mutual aid was organized, where political strategies were developed, where the hungry were fed and the grieving were comforted and the ambitious were encouraged.

The collection plate. The passing of the plate in a Black church is an act with dimensions that transcend its financial function. It is an expression of collective responsibility. It is the community saying, together: we will take care of each other. What you give is returned to you — in the form of the institution that sustains the community, in the form of the programs that serve the vulnerable, in the form of the solidarity that makes survival possible.

The kitchen table. In the tradition of Black hospitality, no one who comes to the door hungry is turned away. This is not policy. It is culture — the expression of a value so deep and so old that it does not require articulation. You share what you have. If you have little, you share a little. If you have much, you share much. The table is set for whoever needs to sit at it.

This is philanthropy. This is love of humanity made practical.

The gift was never withheld.

It was given before it had a name.

It is being given now, in a thousand kitchens and a thousand collection plates and a thousand acts of quiet generosity that will never be recorded in any foundation's annual report but that are the actual substance of what keeps a community alive.

VOTING
RIGHTS
NOW!
БTLP
VOTER
SUPPRESSIS
VOTE

CHAPTER ELEVEN

The Republic Was Never Free

A Tribute to Black Struggle for Democracy

The United States of America was founded on a contradiction. The men who wrote the Declaration of Independence — who declared that all men are created equal, that they are endowed by their Creator with certain unalienable rights, that among these are life, liberty, and the pursuit of happiness — were, many of them, slaveholders. They wrote these words and they meant them, or they thought they meant them, and they enslaved people. They wrote these words and built a nation on the premise that they did not apply to everyone.

This contradiction was not a paradox that paralyzed the founders. It was a managed tension, kept manageable by the decision not to extend the concept of "men" to include Black people. The language was universal. The application was not. And the history of Black American political life is, in its essential form, the history of insisting that the language mean what it says — that the promise be kept, the note be honored, the Declaration be made true.

This is not an effort to reform America from the outside. It is an effort, conducted from within, to make America be what it has always claimed to be. Black Americans have not been asking for something new. They have been demanding something promised. The difference matters.

It means that the Black struggle for democracy is not merely a struggle for Black liberation. It is the struggle for American democracy itself — for the actualization of the principles that the nation claims as its foundation. And every gain that Black Americans have made in this struggle has been a gain for the nation as a whole, whether the nation understood it at the time or not.

Crispus Attucks: The First American Martyr

On March 5, 1770, a crowd of colonists gathered in front of the Custom House on King Street in Boston, confronting a small group of British soldiers. The confrontation had been building for weeks — the soldiers were resented by the colonists, their presence in the city felt as an occupation, their interactions with civilians a daily source of tension.

A man in the front of the crowd was the first to fall when the soldiers fired. His name was Crispus Attucks. He was of mixed African and Native American descent, possibly a formerly enslaved man who had escaped and been living as a sailor and rope-maker. He was approximately forty- seven years old. He died of two musket balls to the chest.

He became, in the mythology of the American Revolution, the first martyr of American liberty. Paul Revere's famous engraving of the "Boston Massacre" depicted the scene, though not accurately — it did not acknowledge Attucks's racial identity, presenting the fallen as undifferentiated Americans. The reality was that the first blood shed in the cause of American independence was Black blood.

The irony is not subtle. The nation that was being born on the proposition that all men are created equal was inaugurated with the death of a Black man who would not, for another century, be counted as fully human by the legal system that that nation created.

Attucks was buried with honors in Boston. His memory was invoked by abolitionists and civil rights advocates in the centuries that followed as evidence that Black people had been present at the creation of the nation — that the argument for Black citizenship was not an argument for something new but a demand for something owed.

He had paid the first price.

The debt was not settled for 200 years.

It is not fully settled yet.

The 54th Massachusetts: Blood as Argument

In 1863, the 54th Massachusetts Infantry — one of the first officially organized Black units in the Union Army — attacked Battery Wagner, a Confederate fortification on Morris Island, South Carolina. The assault was a tactical failure. The regiment suffered devastating casualties: 272 men killed, wounded, or captured, including their commanding officer, Colonel Robert Gould Shaw, who was killed at the top of the parapet.

But the assault was, in a deeper sense, a victory.

It demonstrated, to a Union Army and a Northern public that had been skeptical about Black soldiers' willingness and ability to fight, that Black men would fight and die for the Union with the same courage that white soldiers displayed. Frederick Douglass, whose sons Charles and Lewis were among the regiment's members, had understood from the beginning what was at stake beyond the tactical objective: "Once you let the black man get upon his person the brass letter, U.S., let him get an eagle on his button, and a musket on his shoulder and bullets in his pocket, and there is no power on earth which can deny that he has earned the right to citizenship."

He was right. The service of Black soldiers in the Civil War was one of the most powerful arguments for Black citizenship — not an argument made in words, though those arguments were also being made, but an argument made in blood, in sacrifice, in the willingness to give the last full measure of devotion to a country that had not yet decided to fully claim them.

The 13th, 14th, and 15th Amendments to the Constitution followed. The legal framework for Black citizenship was established. And then, with the end of Reconstruction, the practical reality of that citizenship was systematically dismantled by the violence and legal maneuvering of the former Confederacy and its allies.

The blood had been paid.

The promise was deferred.

The struggle continued.

John Lewis and the Bridge

On March 7, 1965, approximately 600 civil rights marchers set out from Selma, Alabama, planning to march to Montgomery, the state capital, to demand the right to vote.

They had tried once before. Governor George Wallace had sent state troopers to prevent them.

The troopers were waiting at the Edmund Pettus Bridge — a bridge named for a former Grand Dragon of the Ku Klux Klan.

At the head of the march was a young man named John Lewis. He was twenty-five years old. He had grown up in Pike County, Alabama, the son of sharecroppers, had been inspired by the Montgomery Bus Boycott as a teenager, had been training and organizing and participating in the civil rights movement since his late teens, had been beaten and arrested dozens of times.

He led the marchers onto the bridge. The troopers ordered them to turn around. They did not turn around. The troopers attacked. Lewis was struck on the head with a nightstick and fractured his skull. The images of the attack — which became known as Bloody Sunday — were broadcast on national television and shocked a country that had been slow to understand what was happening in the South.

President Johnson introduced the Voting Rights Act within days.

Lewis recovered. He did not stop. He continued marching and organizing and eventually was elected to Congress from Georgia, where he served for thirty-three years, until his death in 2020. He was called the conscience of the Congress. He continued to speak, with a clarity and a gentleness and an unshakable moral authority, about the work that remained to be done.

He said: "Do not get lost in a sea of despair. Be hopeful, be optimistic. Our struggle is not the struggle of a day, a week, a month, or a year, it is the struggle of a lifetime."

He lived the struggle of a lifetime.

He left the work to us.

Stacey Abrams and the New Reconstruction

In 2018, Stacey Abrams ran for governor of Georgia. She lost, in an election marred by widespread voter suppression — the suppression carried out in large part by her opponent, the sitting Secretary of State, who had overseen the purging of hundreds of thousands of voters from the rolls and the closing of polling places in predominantly Black counties.

She did not concede in the traditional sense. She acknowledged the mathematical reality of the outcome.

She did not acknowledge its legitimacy. And then she did something that would prove more consequential than any concession speech: she organized.

She founded Fair Fight Action, an organization dedicated to combating voter suppression. She registered hundreds of thousands of new voters in Georgia — voters who were predominantly Black, who had been systematically discouraged from participating in the democratic process, who were now being sought out and supported and given the practical assistance they needed to exercise the right that John Lewis had nearly died to secure for them.

In January 2021, two Democratic senators were elected from Georgia, flipping the Senate's majority and making possible the legislative agenda of the incoming Biden administration. Both senators won in large part because of the voter mobilization that Abrams and her network had built. One of them, Raphael Warnock, was the pastor of Ebenezer Baptist Church in Atlanta — the church where Martin Luther King Jr. had preached.

The arc of history bent. It did not bend on its own. It bent because people applied force to it — specific, organized, sustained force, in the form of voter registration and legal challenges and community organizing and the patient, unglamorous work of democracy.

Stacey Abrams applied the force.

The arc bent.

The republic was never free.

But it is freer when we fight for it.

And we are always fighting for it.

Epilogue
The Living Spire
The Cathedral Is Never Finished

The Cathedral Is Never Finished

As I set down the pen on this first volume, I am struck by the realization that a foundation is not a conclusion; it is a beginning. We have walked through the long galleries of our ancestors—from the astronomers of Mali to the "Red Tails" who claimed the sky—and in doing so, we have refused the silence that was designed for us. We have looked upon the "sorrow songs" and the "psalms of rage," not merely to mourn, but to inherit the strength that allowed such beauty to grow in such desperate soil.

This manuscript is intended to be a living entity. It is a vessel for the voices that are still rising, the essays yet to be written, and the histories still being unearthed from the archives and the kitchen tables of our elders. I have laid the stones for these first pillars, but the arches must continue to climb.

There will come a time when my hands are no longer the ones to steady the light in this place. I welcome that day.

To the next curator: you do not step into a tomb, but into a pulse. The stories within these pages are not static; they are the "rhythm of footsteps" that continue to echo in every generation that demands dignity.

The work of memory is an eternal vigil. It is the steady beat of the drum that began in the "earth of the Eve gene" and continues in the pulse of our children. May you carry this record with the same "absolute clarity" as those who stood guard before us. Add your own truths. Seek out the erased. Keep the windows clean so that the light of our history never stops illuminating the path forward.

The promise is kept, but the building continues.

About the Author

Tracey Patrick Valmont is an artisan of memory, a nomad of the spirit, and a builder of sanctuaries.

To understand the architecture of this book, one must understand the hands that laid the stones. Tracey's life has been defined not by a single destination, but by a migratory journey — an existence that has moved through the storied streets of London and the quiet corners of the world, never truly finding a home in geography, but always finding one in history. This perspective allowed the author to hear the whispers of the ancestors that others, more settled and comfortable, might have missed.

But every Cathedral is built on hallowed ground, and hallowed ground is often consecrated by struggle.

Tracey writes from a place of radical honesty, electing to place this introduction at the end of the work to ensure the history stands first, while the truth stands last. Set apart by a life that has known the raw, haunting presence of "demons" in the life-lived sense, Tracey has navigated the heavy currents of addiction behind closed doors. These battles were fought with a fierce, southern discretion — not out of a desire to hide, but out of a profound love for those who could never be allowed to witness the offense.

There is no fraud in this struggle. Instead, there is the evidence of a soul that has refused to be defined by its shadows. By exposing the raw edges of a lived experience, Tracey confirms that the Eve Gene is not a myth of perfection, but a reality of endurance. It is the gene that survives the fire, the massacre, the exile, and the addiction, only to rise and build something beautiful again.

Tracey remains a seeker and a migrant, still moving, still listening, and still proving that even a haunted life can reach for the firmament. This Cathedral is the testament of a witness who has walked through the dark to ensure that the light of the ancestors is never extinguished.

✦

The Cathedral of Memory

Volume I

First published 2026 by Grolee House

Opelousas, Louisiana

Set in Garamond

ISBN 979-8-234-04041-1